indiana

winter

susan neville

*indiana
university
press*

bloomington & indianapolis

W9-AXR-327

© 1994 by susan neville

all rights reserved

no part of this book may be reproduced or utilized in any form or by any means, electronic or mechanical, including photocopying and recording, or by any information storage and retrieval system, without permission in writing from the publisher. the association of american university presses' resolution on permissions constitutes the only exception to this prohibition.

the paper used in this publication meets the minimum requirements of american national standard for information sciences—permanence of paper for printed library materials, ansi z39.48-1984.

manufactured in the united states of america

library of congress cataloging-in-publication data

neville, susan.
  indiana winter / susan neville.
    p.   cm.
  isbn 0-253-34004-7 (alk. paper). — isbn 0-253-20879-3 (pbk. : alk. paper)
    1. indiana—literary collections.   I. title.
  ps3564.e8525I47   1994
814'.54—dc20   93-40692

1   2   3   4   5   00   99   98   97   96   95   94

it will be seen

that men

go mad in herds,

while they only

recover their

senses slowly,

and one

by one.

Charles Mackay, from

Extraordinary Popular

Delusions *and the*

Madness of Crowds.

contents

"I don't know how to pray," Mary Oliver says in one of her poems, "but I do know how to pay attention." I took that line as my aesthetic when I began this book—a book I had intended as a collection of prose pieces about Indiana and spiritual icons. I wanted to do something closer to journalism than to fiction or autobiography, something that would focus my eye out onto the world.

What I ended up doing was following my curiosity wherever it took me. I decided to trust it. If I was even the slightest bit curious about something, I barged right into the middle of it—talked to people, took notes. My curiosity took me into prisons and a jail, into country churches, small towns and farms, to the State Fair, the Dillinger Museum in Nashville, John Mellencamp's art opening in Seymour, and to New Harmony on the day of Iben Browning's predicted earthquake.

My curiosity also took me, in ways I didn't realize, and would have guarded against if I'd known, on a road that led right back to myself and my own history—the very thing I was trying to avoid.

I wandered through Indiana with a question that was very quirkily mine, and which, for good or ill, drew certain types of images and stories from the people and the landscape as though it were magnetized.

The question is in many ways still confusing to me, but it runs something like this: I grew up in Indianapolis, in a middle-class, suburban family, in a neighborhood of other middle-class, suburban families. My mother and father were very loving and very kind. My mother was also manic-depressive, a grand weaver of delusions. So in some of these pieces, as much as they're about high school gyms and car dealerships and sycamores, there's a concern with the difference between story-telling and delusion-weaving, and the difference between private and public madness. My mother's illness made me very aware of the difference between literal and metaphorical truth. It also made me very conscious of things that are hidden, of all kinds of silences. I include the personal essay "In the Suburbs" to help mark the place where the external landscape is filtered through my personal one.

I should say too that I play fast and loose with genre definitions in these pieces. Many of them occupy some gray border area between the short story, personal essay, and journalism.

Some days all I had to do was pay attention to the people and the places around me and, simply, report. "Nineveh" and "Quake" are two obvious examples. The towns of Nineveh and New Harmony wrote those two essays—every detail and bit of conversation. I eavesdropped shamelessly in crowds in order to get a sense of what people were thinking and saying when they weren't self-conscious, as they usually are when they know they're being interviewed. Of course then I often had to fictionalize details in order to protect people's privacy.

Four of the pieces—"Jubilee," "The Garden City Church of Christ," "The Problem of Evil," and "In the John Dillinger Museum"—are short stories. I invented characters that fit my sense of a place as seen through a mind I had no legitimate way of approaching except through fiction. The "I" narrator in Jubilee is the only "I" narrator I wouldn't claim is me. I think of the collection as a meditation about a place as seen through the lens of my own questions. I hope that the stories and essays echo one another and that the questions raised by the juxtaposition of the imagined and the observed become part of the meditation.

I'd like to thank those people who have helped me with this book: my husband, Ken, and children, Steven and Laura; my friends and readers Jean Anaporte, John Gallman, Michael Martone, Jim Watt, Kathleen O'Fallon, Grace Farrell, Andrew Levy, Susan and Michael Sutherlin, Kent Calder, Tom Emery, Dale Hathaway, Margaret Brabant, Craig Auchter, and Scott Russell Sanders.

And finally: My mother died last spring, six weeks almost to the day after my grandmother. This book is dedicated to their memory and to my mother's courage.

acknowledgments

"Stone" and "Garden City Church of Christ" appeared in *Painted Bride Quarterly*. "Indiana Winter" and "The Problem of Evil" appeared in *The Sycamore Review*. "In the John Dillinger Museum" appeared in *The Sycamore Review* and *Pushcart Prize XIV: Best of the Small Presses*. "Whirligig!" appeared in *Ambergris*, "Nineveh" in *Traces*. "Jubilee" and "Hey John" appeared in *Arts Indiana*. "Quake" was published in *Townships*. "The Tent" first appeared in *Crazyhorse* and was reprinted in *The Hopewell Review*. "Seeds" appeared in the *Mid-American Review* and "In the Suburbs" in *Boulevard*. An earlier version of "Prisoners" was published in *The North American Review*.

indiana

winter

s t o n e

My home is a harbor. It floats on limestone high above the Ohio. Underneath our
feet, acids eat away the stone and there are underground rivers and caves and, I swear it, if
you were small enough and didn't mind tight
black places, darker than any dark you could
imagine, and you could crawl through slime
and rushing water through tunnels that could
end with any step in a cavern so deep you
would never stop falling, if you didn't mind
knowing that could happen at any moment, if
the thought of cave-ins and earthquakes does
not concern you because you somehow carry

yourself with you gently as a baby, you could be the first person to crawl from Indiana to the brightly lit caverns in Kentucky.

And imagine it, after years of groping, how like heaven it would seem to you, emerging in even the tackiest tent-colored cavern lit with red and blue and green floodlights, seeing a man with a flashlight aiming it at the ceiling—saying doesn't this look like draperies, doesn't that rock look like bacon frying, doesn't that one look like an elf, here in the body of the earth isn't nature a miracle, millions of years ago, making a rock that looks like a toaster?

And still we float so gently on this gloom, in the graying yellow October daylight, in the night lit with candles, in the strong wood houses and barns, in the orchards where the apples fall into our hands and the leaves twist down. We sail on the land as though it's real, our compasses pointing north, as though we know where we are. We eat sugar pears and watch the sugar maples blaze and we suck on sweet candy and smell the damp decaying leaves, and we hold on tight as the boat heaves or the land pitches.

indiana winter

It's the dead of winter. A landlocked state. Seven cars maneuver between frozen bean fields under gray skies. Seven men drive. Six women hold warm casseroles wrapped in towels.

Each car pushes its own small horn of light, scraping the road and frozen waves of soil until it blends with the others in the dim floodlights of one driveway.

The men and women leave their cars and go to the front door of a farmhouse. The women hug the casseroles. The men stand behind them. Their breath plumes as they wait.

Inside there is movement! Noise! Bright light! A party, hot spiced tea on the stove. Divinity! Take the casseroles in the kitchen, the hostess says, pile the coats on the bed.

The guests move into the large kitchen, into the brick-walled family room, around the wood stove, past the rack of shining guns. Some of the women stay in the kitchen and arrange dishes. The one old man stays with them. He stands at the kitchen counter with a toothed knife and homemade bread. His spotted hands make precise cuts. The rest of the men and some of the women move close to the basketball game on the television.

The women talk about their children. Some of the men talk about money. A million dollars at retirement, a banker says, guaranteed. Honey, a woman yells to her husband, listen to this. Her husband has gone in the kitchen with the host to inspect a leaking pipe. The wealth we could have when we retire, she thinks. Honey, imagine, the security. There's a roar around the flickering television. Damnit, Uwe, the host booms, coming back from the kitchen, you were wide open. If I had been that tall, he says, I'd own the damn state and throw in Kentucky.

We're ready, the hostess calls. Come. Eat.

Glass casseroles, clouds of steam. Yams

sweet in orange sauce. Almond cookies. Home-canned beans, red tomatoes, ham. Yeast breads, risen. Sugar pies. Cranberry ice in pink glasses. Paper plates stamped with holly. There is no wine. Taste. Shh. The host. Please, give us grace. The clatter of silver on glass. The flash of fire from knives, candle flames cradled in spoons. Your bread, Reverend, is delicious. Outside the house, the frost line is two feet deep. A rabbit run over by a car, its fur frozen. Inside the house, the air is as thick and warm and yellow as clotted cream. If only we lived here, the guests believe, we would never be unhappy.

She bought the skirt to wear tonight, but the waist button is already tight. She had no idea it would happen so fast. Under the table, her husband's knee presses hers. Still their secret, the child curled like a spoon under the paper napkin. Conceived in the dead of winter, lucky child, the mother hopes. Less danger of miscarriage than those children begun in the season of dogwood and iris, red discing, herbicide and dust. Half the women here seem cloudy with never-born children. There was that spring when three of the women miscarried in April. At the end of nine months, one had said, she felt the child's presence like a phantom limb.

Last spring it had happened to her too.

The three months of growth, then the blood, then the waiting, then this new baby who would always feel like two. Later that spring there had been the fragile green of early corn, the good, kind faces of farmers in town, and no real connection between anything.

The candles carve out the slight hollows underneath her husband's cheekbones, the cold glow of early silver in his hair. Husband, do you know how much I love you? Sometimes this world seems so temporary. The whole table laughs at something the host has said. Her husband looks ecstatic. Life is wonderful, she knows he is thinking, marvelous. Husband, I'm frightened. Do you know how much I love you?

The Reverend's hand is dry on the pink water glass. His lips are unsteady. He sees the exhilaration on the face of the young man beside him. The young man turns to him, out of politeness says And for Christmas, Reverend, where will you be? The Reverend says he's not sure yet and the young man looks for a second guiltily at his wife until the Reverend says he has several offers and the husband relaxes and touches his wife's hand.

I hope, she says, this holiday won't be difficult for you, and the Reverend says Oh no, I'm going to try to keep busy. I read a lot, you know.

He starts to tell them about an Eskimo book he's been reading, forgetting the vows he had made as a young man when old retired uncles would talk endlessly at family dinners about birds or former presidents, the vows that he would never bore young people like that. But the pleasure of conversation! Of hearing himself tell someone about the things he's filled his mind with — ice houses and frozen seals and lamps of fat and hot tea. Though it seems to come out odd. For a moment he feels dizzy, like that kayak sickness when the sky and water are such a blinding blue and white that you can't tell up from down.

The host's face and neck are as red as sunburn. He shouts across two women. The game should have started. A father with a son on the team looks up nervously from his plate, a cookie in his hand. You think so? He's been aware of every minute. Yes, it's time. The host reaches for a radio on the table behind him. His wife looks at him, and he doesn't turn it on.

The basketball player's father thinks of the drive back through the country to town. Hundreds of gravestones along the highway leading to the fieldhouse. On Saturday nights, when the traffic gets heavy, the gravestones snap with sharp, reflected light, like rows of cameras aimed right for his son.

The fieldhouse is a sea of green sweat-
shirts by now. Teenagers cruise the perimeter
in two concentric circles, their eyes head-
lights. Scoreboards flashing, steamed eye-
glasses, candy wrappers, old men and babies.
Everyone in town is there, and his son! The
father looks up to see if anyone's looking at
him. He takes another cookie. My God, his
son. Legs like a racehorse, just as fast. Only a
sophomore, but already some people know.
The old Reverend knows, the way he clasps the
boy's hand on the Sundays they bring him out
of retirement to preach, the way he leans forward in his thin tie and white shirt, his hands
on his knees, focusing always on his son as in-
tently as he, the father, focuses. Everyone in
town is unemployed or just holding on, waiting for something. And it's his son. Never
misses a free throw. Hits from halfway down
the court. But still inconsistent, young. Not everyone knows what he'll be: best point guard
in the state, in the country. Records that will
stand. He has a gift. Everyone is waiting for
something, and it's his son they're waiting for.

He holds his own small hand a few inches
above the table, looks at the top, then the
palm. Where did he come from, his son? A
game tonight, and he let his wife talk him into
missing it for this party. Already he's regretting
that he's come. This party, she said, I look forward all year. A game tonight.

The host jumps up, says To the best cooks in the county. A toast with this piece of fudge. He picks up the radio and heads for the family room. One by one the men follow, scraping chairs, joking. The old Reverend and the young husband stay behind, helping the women clear dishes. The cold presses against the bay window by the table, comes down the chimney in the living room by the tree.

Start another fire, the hostess says.

There is the sound of basketball from the family room, the odor of wood burning in the stove and the fireplace, of smoke from the snuffed-out candles. The women's faces are glowing from the warmth, stomachs round as bubbles.

When the old man runs out of things he can see to do and stands with his hands at his sides, the women send him into the family room and begin comparing childbirth stories. They all know each other's stories but pretend, for the pleasure of telling them again. Labor started in the car, in the bathroom, in bed, at work, in the grocery. Tipped uterus, dilated cervix, placenta praevia, I was so scared. Four children, says one woman, and they were all a breeze; I could do it every day. Twenty hours of labor, says another, I almost died. Forty-eight hours for me, says another.

The young husband helping with the

dishes goes into the living room to stand by the fire.

I knew right away when I was pregnant, one woman says, my breasts so sore I couldn't sleep on them. With Todd, another says, I was on the pill for two months and didn't know; when I found out, I worried the whole time.

They outdo one another with horror stories, secondhand, and casually told. A child born without ears, stillborn children wrapped in magazines at the foot of a teenager's bed. A two-pound baby born too early who fits in the palm of her mother's hand.

Slowly they bring up their own worries. A child who doesn't crawl. A boy who cries at night. A baby who hasn't yet turned over—Mine didn't turn until he was ever so old, the hostess says, and now he's gifted. One woman's daughter with leukemia, in remission, her lips so dry in the hospital the mother rubbed them with the strawberry lip gloss she sells door to door, a beautiful child. They'll be well, the women reassure one another, they all will be well. Remember the way a baby's soft hair feels on your cheek, the way you hate to give up nursing.

The woman in the wool skirt wants to tell but is afraid to bring bad luck. Some days, she thinks, it feels like a festival, and some days I'm so frightened. The hostess takes powdered cream from a shelf and pours it into a small pitcher with a silver spoon. She turns to the woman in the wool skirt who has nothing to add to the conversation. Now which grade is it you teach again? The woman in the wool skirt answers, smiles, goes into the living room to find her husband.

The husband and wife stand in the living room by the tree. How do you feel? he asks her. She smiles and looks into the tree: planets and stars brought inside against the winter. She lets her eyes lose focus and leans into her husband, galaxies of lights multiplied and spinning, filling the room, her husband's body the only stable, unchanging thing in a universe too large, the tiny child the size of her thumb. A log cracks and falls through the fireplace grate, an explosion of orange sparks. He puts his arm around her waist. I never realized it, she says, for so long, how people have had the courage to have children.

The temperature drops below zero. The wind blows dark branches of evergreens outside the windows. The women see the branches and move into the family room. The husband and wife hear the wind and move into the family room. The men are laughing at something they can't explain.

The old Reverend sits uncomfortably in the best overstuffed chair. When he sees the couple come in from the living room, he offers it to the woman and moves to a stiff, wooden one.

Please, he thinks. Listen to me. For months my house has been darker than I remember it ever being, the outside gray seeping in and nothing I do will keep it out. The northern winters that last six months, a warm light from seal fat shining through ice and one family living by itself until the air gets close and then running miles through the black cold to another place just like it, all ice and dark, and a new house in hours, the universe shrunk to a bright warm dot. If my house could feel as warm as that, as warm as this place, please listen.

The host opens the wood-burning stove. The room seems smaller. Maybe it will snow, someone says. Not a chance, says the basketball player's father. It only snows in March during basketball play-offs. Right now it's the middle of the gray season, not a chance for snow.

The hostess passes pecans in the shell. The host picks up a book from the coffee table. He shows it to the woman in the wool skirt. The inscription reads "to my friend." It was signed by the author. The cover is bright yellow with orange. We were in Vietnam together, the host says. He shot himself after the book was published. The host says this with bravado, his knees spread wide.

Pecan shells cracking dust in the air. Black windows sweating. We got lost coming here, the woman says to him, ended up by the grain elevators.

They are the host's elevators, round white silos. In the fall farmers bring him their crops. In the spring he sells them poisons.

The woman remembers high school, another party. She didn't know anyone there. She'd gone with a boy she wasn't supposed to even talk to. Most of the boys she knew were college-bound and not worried. This was one of the expendable ones. There was nothing he wanted to do with his life, no job worth waiting for, probably no job at all.

She can't remember how she got there, whose car they went in. It was a frame working-class house close to other houses just like it. They all had porches. There were no adults, or rather, no authority. Someone's older brother was there.

There were a lot of people in the living room. She remembers orange-flowered upholstery, a windowsill covered with chips of putty and paint, the shells of bugs. She doesn't remember faces. The older brother had short hair. He was home on some sort of leave. He laughed hard, his arm crooked around the neck of a short, long-haired girl. It was like he was choking her.

He got out a white screen and set it up against a wall. He had a case of slides. The projector was old and the slides kept sticking. It bothered him when one of the slides was in backward, though no one else could tell. She thinks she remembers him laughing as he showed them but doesn't trust that memory. She turned away from the screen.

And what does that have to do with this room, earthy nut taste, lingering cinnamon and cranberry, hot coffee, her child. The host and that boy pulled out of the county, her future husband sitting safe in an accounting class. Just from watching the news, she says now to the host, even to me, there's something terrifying about helicopters.

We're living in dark times, the host says, and she nods.

Dark times, the host says, and the men agree. Smoke from pipes and one or two cigarettes. The largest all-brick factory in the world, now a quiet old fossil in the center of town. Windows are broken out and covered with paper. Acres of empty parking lots full of trash. There are For Sale signs in every neighborhood, many of them foreclosures. Last fall a stomping death out by the county high school. Of course the banks are holding on, one or two of the furniture stores. Churches are still open, the children at school dreaming about the future. The hostess passes ribbon candy.

She goes to an exercise class twice a week in the basement under the B&G Gym. The class is downtown, near the courthouse, and most of the stores around it are empty, the windows blank. The basement is unfinished: block walls, bare bulb lights, a slanting, cracked concrete floor with rusted drains, years of dust and cobwebs, exposed pipes and supporting beams holding up the gym floor. The children play to the side, by the furnace, on a tumbling mat. It's a dreary place to be but the only other exercise class, which meets in the new, light-filled gym behind the Baptist church, where prayer concerns precede each session and a head of Christ fills one whole wall in a paint-by-numbers style, has no provision for children and meets at an inconvenient time.

The instructor brings a small tape player with tapes of rock music and routines she drives to Indianapolis every other month to learn and they all jump and dance and breathe while overhead men drop hundred-pound weights on an old plank floor and the women imitate their clumsy instructor and watch their children play and pray for grace.

In town, the fieldhouse is packed. The crowd roars as the boys run through the tunnel and onto the floor. The radio announcers interview the mascot, a Roman soldier. An Indian from the visiting school runs around the outside of the court with a tomahawk and the home crowd boos. The soldier walks across the floor on his hands.

The Reverend stares at the radio, trying to picture that tall, confident boy. Sitting on the bench probably while the others start to practice, his head between his hands, praying most likely. Some coaches would mind, but this is a town where the prayer at last year's graduation turned into a revival, with the seniors who thought they were saved raising their hands and shouting.

The Reverend has known that boy since he was born. They were neighbors. He and his wife would sit out on the porch and watch him play. He can remember the boy during that cute toddler stage, when he'd come over to their porch tangling his fingers together and holding his fists up to him as a gift; this is a flower, he'd say, and then untangle them and twist them back together as a star or a bird that only he could see. This is a church, the Reverend would say, showing the boy his own hands and conventional patterns, and this the steeple.

He was like their child. Sometimes he en-

vied the boy's parents but would never say that
to his wife. They had both accepted their in-
ability to have children and had not looked
back. But it amazed him now when he thinks
about it how much of their time they spent
watching this boy, how much of their time they
spent talking about him. His wife worried
when she heard that metallic ringing of the
basketball on the concrete driveway in all
kinds of weather, the boy unable to let himself
come in until he made 100 shots in a row, starting over if he missed one, even in cold rain.

Last year during the closest thing Methodists ever had to a revival, on the fifth night of
services when the minister had asked for the
fifth time for people to come forward in reded-
ication and everyone but two or three old
women who had sat still all their lives and were
tired of it stayed, as usual, politely in their
seats, the boy had come forward and taken the
pulpit, quietly, *quietly*, and with dignity, chas-
tising the congregation for their lack of fervor.

And first his parents had come forward,
his mother crying and his father large and uncomfortable kneeling at the altar, and then the
teenagers and then the others around the parents' age, the ones here tonight, and then most
of the rest, only a small ring of the ever-polite
left sitting on the oak benches at the perimeter.

Dark times, the host says, and the men
and one or two women talk about nuclear war.

Within the next decade, the host says, and some of the men agree. There's no way it won't happen. These are end times, a teacher says, and he begins enumerating the seven horsemen, forgetting four. The host, excited, remembers one—famine. It's like the seven dwarves, the teacher says, any group can only usually remember part of them, and I'm sure there are more. But I think there may only be four, a woman says. How many, Reverend? she asks. There are four horsemen of the apocalypse, he says; but I can't believe it has much to do with this.

At any rate, the host says, you have to believe it's true, within the decade. A banker agrees. The economy is falling apart, he says, you know this year the bank didn't hold its Christmas party. And it's happening everywhere. That always comes before war. We can't live with this tension anymore, sooner or later one of us, maybe even it will be us, will decide to hell with it and start the whole thing going.

It could happen by accident, one of the women says.

And probably will, says the host.

Maybe we'll be safe out here, the hostess says.

An accountant who had just read an article in a magazine shakes his head. One of the newer missiles hits Indianapolis, Chicago, or Dayton, and we've all had it.

Why would anyone aim at those cities, a woman asks; they're not New York or Washington.

The Russians will want to save the Rockettes, the banker says—and anyway, who had ever heard of Nagasaki?

Summer, gray-green jets from Wright Patterson practice maneuvers over the farmhouse while the hostess hangs out laundry. They fly so fast she would miss them if it weren't for the sound. Her youngest boy hides under a red maple. When the planes fly back into the morning sun they turn white and fragile as tiny, brittle bones.

She excuses herself and goes into the kitchen for more coffee. When she comes back to the party she sits on the other side of the room where a few of the women are huddled around a table.

According to this article, the accountant says, you can make a quick shelter against the foundation of your house, kind of like a deep window well—that is, if you have an hour or so warning, and if you're far enough away that all you have to worry about is fallout. Sounds like a grave, says a banker. You can survive fallout, the husband of the woman in the wool skirt says. At least for a day or two, says the host.

He's already got twenty-eight points, the father says to the room, and the game's only half over.

I've got my wife drying vegetables, the host says, and we've got ammunition for all those guns. You'd let all of us in, wouldn't you, says the banker with a cane. If we had enough, the host says, looking uncomfortable. We have a lot of friends.

The school record is forty-eight, and he's only a sophomore, says the father.

The host shifts position in his chair and looks at the banker. Of course we'd let you in, he says.

The other banker says he put an electric fence around his place last summer. He cracks a pecan into his handkerchief. The shock waves from one missile in a strategic place, says the accountant, will knock out all the electricity, all the computers, all the cars, everything.

The world's going up in flames, says the host, there aren't any leaders anymore that aren't idiots. Look at our last mayoral election, the teacher says — well-meaning alcoholics and bag ladies and a couple of addicts, the biggest qualification for the job that they're unemployed and have plenty of time to devote to it. Anyone with something to do, a business or family, wouldn't want the job, the banker with the fence says. Not much hope in it.

It's funny, the husband says, looking away from the radio. The day of the big train wreck in Dunreith the plaster cracked in every room in our house, the sky was red from the fire. I woke up and for a minute I was terrified, sure that the Russians had finally dropped the bomb on us. I never stopped to ask why they would choose a town of ten or twelve families and three antique stores as a target. I was sure, the fear so deep in me. At any time, depending on your mood, the most likely two targets seem to be exactly where you are or exactly where you aren't.

If I'm really quiet, his wife thinks, maybe I can feel him move. She stretches her legs out, listens to the logs in the fire and the pleasant crackling of the radio, glad the Reverend gave her the chair in the middle of the men where she can just listen to the drone of their voices, not feeling like she needs to join in the conversation the way she would if she were with the women. She can sit there feeling secret and warm, as though she's the only one this has ever happened to. It will be a boy. She's sure of that already. She and her husband and the boy will come together so tightly they will never need anyone else, never be afraid of anything, never lonely. They will live forever.

One of the women brings a plate of Christmas cookies into the family room and puts it on the coffee table. The host notices the gold lights above the mantel aren't plugged in, and he turns them on. The accountant eats a green-sugared bell, a banker a silver wreath with cinnamon hearts. Dark times, the men agree. They're silent and then turn uncomfortably to the women. The teacher clears his throat, says Well anyway, tell us about the new retirement accounts, and the bankers produce calculators and sheets of paper to prove how if you start now you really could be a millionaire when you retire.

The accountant and the host go into the basement to inspect some new wiring. The ball player's father eats a piece of vanilla fudge. The skin above his sweater is purple. A quiet repairman talks about the deck he's building on the back of his house, the banker with a fence asks him about a leak in his hot water heater.

The room is cold, the light dimming. They all notice the Reverend, poor thing, sitting with his eyes milky, missing his wife.

The basketball player's mother leans forward in her chair, catching the eye of her husband. My God! he shouts and jumps up from his chair. Forty-four points. What's the record? a woman asks. I think it's forty-eight, says the repairman. A nervous excitement bubbles up like tree lights. The accountant and the host come back up from the basement. The banker stops talking about his hot water heater. The women get up from the table and squeeze onto sofas next to their husbands. Three or four men and women sit on the floor. They all face the radio, their backs to the windows.

Who set the record?

Scott Lewis in '68. Maybe Troy Schweikart in '57.

It was Scott, says the Reverend, in '67.

How could I let her talk me out of being there? thinks the father. He stands up and paces.

Thousands of people are crowded into the fieldhouse, others around radios, late on one of the darkest nights of the year. And his son, her son, takes the ball down the floor and from twenty feet outside right through the net without hitting the rim, their son, so quiet when I carried him, where did he come from? The arc of the basketball beginning at a point deep in all of their chests, this boy they know, who is part of them, the arc ending, how could it be otherwise, in the sweet center of the basket, a record set years ago by a boy two years older and, with a foul shot, on this night quietly broken.

The host takes a deep breath of pine from the roping on the mantel. The heat from the crowded room. Dark times, he repeats without thinking, everyone excited, including the host, congratulating the father, who is hugging his wife and hugging the other wives and his friends, a great party. The host slaps one of the bankers on the back. End times.

The woman in the wool skirt touches her husband's hand. Life is wonderful, he thinks, marvelous. Are you ready? she asks. Yes, it's late.

A crowding in the kitchen. Was that your casserole? It was delicious. Don't forget the spoon. Smooth satin lining on coats, voices like bells. The old man with his hands in his pockets hesitates at the door.

Four older model cars and three new ones head into the black night. For a while the house lights blaze. Then the host and hostess turn off the outside lights and turn and lock the doors. And the fields, the trees, the faces in the cars, fade into the winter night.

w h i r l i g i g !

We drive into the country, and it swallows us whole. See that pine? Merle asks. My grand-mother planted it in 1902. My grandparents are buried right over there, he says, and we fly by the dark field he points to so fast we can't see a thing.

This is a great road on a motorcycle, he says. I used to go 80 miles an hour, even on ice. It felt like I was floating.

I sit in the back seat of the car with my eyes closed. Merle's wife is in the front, with her eyes wide open. What happened to the mo-torcycle? I ask.

Got rid of it, he says. I bought an airplane.

What happened to the airplane?

Frances said I spent too much time and money at the airport. We were building the house and needed money.

You two built the house yourself?

All of it except the stonework on the outside.

Where did you live when you were building the house?

In the house, he says. We still haven't finished the upstairs.

How long have you lived there?

Forty years.

Why haven't you finished it?

Got busy with other things.

Do you miss the plane?

I loved flying, he says. And he takes the twisting roads at what feels like 90. You can't make him slow down, Frances says.

He flies around a switchback curve and over a small bridge.

Two preachers went off the side of this bridge, he says, and died.

At the same time? I ask.

No. Different preachers, two different times.

I hunker down in the seat and hope that it's some sort of rogue angel bridge, a black hole that raptures perfect souls to God. And it

must be. Like a turnstile, it flings us out of Bar-
tholomew County.

Planes and trucks, bees and clover, catfish,
orchard, cider press. I'm a jack-of-all-trades,
Merle said before we left his house, a master of
none. Right now he's into gospel singing and
whirligigs. He's bought an organ and a piano
and tape player, and put together a quartet
with his wife and their two sisters. It will be
something different in a year or two, can't stay,
just passing through.

When he was younger, he sang with his
dad and sisters in a quartet. We had an orchestree, he said to me. Orchestree? Orches-
traaaahh, he said then, for my sake.

His voice lay fallow for years. Then his sister heard him sing bass, and they started singing at his church. They went to a hymn sing
and thought "we could do that." Don't expect
a lot from the hymn sing tonight, he said to
me. Television's ruined things like that, he said.
Used to be every country church would have
its star, and now you can tune in to the best
voices in the world on any night.

I've been told that Merle can do anything,
that there is no gift, aside from the gift of making money, that he doesn't have. Before he retired, he was one of the county's best mechan-
ics. Something breaks down on the tractor,

someone said to me, and Merle can fashion a part sometimes it seems like out of thin air. You can tell what Merle's into now, someone else said, by looking at that acre of land in front of his house. Since I've known him, he's had a u-pick strawberry patch there, an acre of irises, an orchard, rows of grape vines, and an acre of clover and white beehives. A couple of years ago he dug a lake out behind the house and stocked it with catfish. Some of them are thirty inches long now, hundreds of catfish that boil up to the surface when they hear him coming with his sack of feed; they feel the vibration of his step.

One summer he made cider with a hand-crank press. Another one he spent cruising estate sales, looking for whiskey bottles, even though he himself drinks nothing but milk and water. The entire back room of his house is filled with dusty bottles. Every wall is covered, ceiling to floor, with them. Ceramic turkeys, ceramic cars, ceramic horses. Ornate gilded bottles, a whole row of blue glass bottles shaped like fiddles. In any set where he's missing one, there's a gap between bottles where the missing one will go. Some of the decanters come with a brood of matching glasses. I took a cranberry red one down to look at it and, when I put it back, I didn't set it far enough away from the shelf's edge. When the guns go

off at Camp Atterbury, he said, this whole
room starts shaking. Now and then a glass falls
off the edge and breaks.

There was a paper hornet's nest draped
like last winter's coat on top of an old couch in
the bottle room. I remember that I'd seen a
couple more in the living room when I came in.
They were hanging in the corners on the dried
leaf-covered twigs they'd been formed on. He
has, he told me, eleven of them now; it's another of his hobbies. Why? Something in you
says you have to do it, so you do.

Right now a large part of his day goes into
making whirligigs out of two-litre plastic
bottles—one of those who'd-ever-think-it craft
projects that spreads from one part of the
country to another. You make angular cuts all
around the bottom of the bottle and flare them
out. It whirls in the slightest wind. He'd put his
own spin on it, invented a machine that would
make all the cuts at once. He painted some of
the bottles white, glued a plastic baseball on
the top, discovered that he could melt the edge
of a piece of black PVC pipe and curve it up for
the brim of a stovepipe hat. There's a troop of
whirling snowmen on the steps. He has an
American flag whirligig, a giddy St. Patrick's
Day green one, and one covered with rows of
perfect hearts.

He sells them at estate sales and flea markets. He'll have a handful of whirling two-litre bottles, like a balloonman. Sometimes he sells baskets of plums, or, in the fall, chrysanthemums. When he had a plane, he flew out to Oklahoma to hunt rattlesnakes, and he sold the skins.

When his kids were young, he started a little league for country kids down the road in someone's then-government-subsidized field. He mowed off the field the farmer was being paid not to plant, built the diamonds and elaborate backstops. One year there were two teams so good that they played each other twice a week clear through the fall. People would drive out from town to see them. He's an ecstatic, a man of sudden enthusiasms and sudden tempers. Like a dervish, or a Shaker.

He has a brother who was a chalk evangelist. What's that? I asked, and he explained it's someone without a home who goes from church to church preaching and drawing—so quick, like a magician—what the spirit directs him to. An artist? Yes, he said, an artist, and it turns out that of course Merle himself can draw. A local school used to pay him to draw poinsettias on the chalkboards at Christmas. He's not bragging when he tells me this or when he takes me into another room to see the one and only drawing he had ever finished in his life. He knew he could do it, so why do more? It's the only drawing and it is, in fact, very beautiful and very strange, with blue shadows and a thin red line of light around the trees, a red like the one you see between your fingers when you cup them over a flashlight. Babies have that same outline of light, he said, you look for it. He doesn't brag, takes no credit for his gifts, is only gleeful to have found another one.

It's not an ordinary thing for anyone to buy an airplane when he's working full-time on an assembly line and at the same time doing some farming and repair work and at the same time has a wife and two kids and an unfinished house. It took an Olympic-quality feat of the imagination.

We flew out to Santa Fe, New Mexico, he told me. Some guy picked us up at the airport; he thought we were rich. If they think you're rich, they treat you like kids. We didn't touch nothin—he took our bags, opened all the doors for us. He was expectin a $10 or $15 tip. Frankie says "he wants a tip," and I said I'm not gonna give him no tip. He makes his money just like I do.

Did you enjoy it? I asked Frances, wondering what it feels like to attach yourself voluntarily and permanently to a whirl of completely unpredictable energy.

Frankie watched that airplane more than I

did, Merle volunteered. She was always sayin don't you think we should stop for gas, doesn't that engine sound funny?

Once the alternator went out, he said, and all the power.

We were flying over Hazard. It's rough country down there, and we couldn't see anything.

Our radio went out, all our instruments, and so I flew to Lexington by watchin the beacon light. Frankie was lyin on the floor, under my sheepskin coat.

That's exactly what I'd do, I said, just get under a coat and pretend you're in your living room.

I figured the windows would break when we crashed, Frances said. And I'd be away from the breaking glass.

We landed in the dark, Merle said. I couldn't see the runway, but it was the best landing I ever made in my life.

If you're maybe gonna kill yourself, he says, you might as well keep from killing yourself. You don't just throw your hands in the air and panic.

They went to Germany a couple of years ago to visit a son who's in the military. It was the first time he'd been in a plane since he sold his. The plane, he said, was the best part of the trip.

The brakes went out on his rental car

while he was in Europe, and he drove from It-
aly to Germany pulling on the emergency
brake whenever he needed to stop.

When I got back, he said, I told the guys I
wouldn't trade Indiana for ten Germanies.

His problem was, Frances said, that he
couldn't talk to anybody over there, and you
know he loves to talk.

There was a model train on a shelf above
his head, an Agatha Christie novel on the floor
beside him, a hornet's nest suspended in the
air. You know we weren't made, Merle said, to
fight against our natures.

The night air smells like dank and weedy
fields, like crushed glass wrecks, metallic
drums and gloom. A small church with its
burning windows and dusky lamps, with its
glittering white gravel, rises up and floats on
top of it. Merle stops the car, and the three of
us get out. There are no other buildings close
by. There's nothing here but the church, not a
thing.

We're late. We go inside and join the others. *This is a new church,* Frances whispers to
me. *A big wind blew the old one down.* Big
wind she says, not tornado, and throughout
the night I hear others say it, a big wind like
the breath of God. (The wind knocked the old
church down so that we could build this new
one. How else can you explain it? There are

photographs, beside the front door, of the old wooden church in the days before the storm. Like a papery old man. You can see for your-self how fragile it was.)

We sit in front. The benches are light oak, the windows a greeny-blue with bubbles that fo-cus light so that it looks like beaded rainwater. On the wall behind the real water of the baptis-mal pool there's a hand-painted river, a symbol once then twice removed, the wet plunge and then the endless rush of the imaginary one.

The congregation sings. *Are your gar-ments spotless? Are they white as snow? Are you washed in the blood of the lamb?*

A thin, serious man in his early seventies is the master of ceremonies. His name is Don, and everyone seems to know him. After the first hymn, he stands up to speak. This is a cold bad time of the year when there's not much goin on, but there are sixty-four here at the Jackson County Hymn Sing!

I pray you'll receive a blessing from this night.

Paul's the first soloist. He's in his late eighties, thin as a bean. He walks up to the po-dium, adjusts his hearing aid, and scowls at us. He plays an old electric guitar that isn't plugged in. There's no resonance. It has a tinny echoless sound. He opens a blue binder filled with yellowed lyrics. How many you want me to sing, Don. I've got enough songs in this book to run about forty-five minutes.

Don tells him he can sing two. Paul coughs into a handkerchief. This is the song, he says, I won my plaque on at the Indiana Gospel Music Association. *I need no mansion here below / Cause Jesus told me I could go / To a home beyond the clouds not made by hands.*

This next one, he says, is dedicated to all railroaders. Any railroaders in the house? Don't believe nary a one. Remember: Christ is your conductor on this lightning train of life.

His voice is as thin and quavering as smoke, but he pushes through the song and ends as elaborately as he began. We watch him pack up the guitar and store it beside the choir loft. We watch him close up the blue binder and walk slowly away from the altar. Everything stops while he does this; our attention wanders. It's like one of those complete silences on the radio when someone's goofed and you think you've lost the station.

Finally he's seated with the rest of us, and a small church choir gets up to sing.

There are ten or so men and women, and they stand in a row near the baptismal pool. The women wear knit slacks and sweaters, the men the same, everyone in brown or gray or green. If I call attention to myself, their eyes say, I might become a lightning rod.

They sing from the hymnal without looking up and without harmony.

Every hymn was written at the turn of the century. Every one is a personal-sin-and-blood-and-earthly-suffering song with the reward far and after death and contingent on the expression of unquestioning faith. I look through the rest of the hymnal, and it's the same thing, all of the hymns written within the twenty-year span between 1890 and 1910 — that time of great malaise, of smallpox and diphtheria and cholera and infant deaths, of the move to the city with its clocks and watches and its overheated rooms, with its specializations and industries, with its deaths confined to hospitals and funeral homes and its slaughter confined to slaughterhouses and its insane and poor and old in institutions and its workers out here in Ratliff Grove (the divisive classifying type of reason that soothes and orders and denies). Every song in the hymnal is mournful. There's no *A Mighty Fortress Is Our God,* no *For the Beauty of the Earth.* The only life is the one that begins at the end.

The message of the Christian mystics, of the Tao, is always the same. That the Kingdom of God is now, in this life, right here on this earth. All you need to do is get out of its way and feel it rushing through you. That's not the Christ who's worshiped in Jackson County. Where they know that there's a grief that curves so endlessly you never see the edge of it. The ways of God are mysterious, and it can be perilous when the wind blows.

A man named Dave, a lay preacher in a gray business suit, gets up to sing. He has a glossy acoustic guitar with a walnut finish; it's the same deep shade of brown as his tinted glasses. He's balding, a little younger than the others. I want my Lord to be satisfied with me, he sings.

Thank you Dave, Don says, and he brings his wife Edna to the piano. We'll try to do something at this time, he says.

Edna starts *Rock of Ages,* and the host begins to speak. He always does this, Frances says. *Jesus,* Don begins, *this is Jimmy.*

And he begins to tell a story over the music, about a young boy in a cold urban landscape. *Mom and Dad loved the nightlife / Jimmy was too much bother. He lived in the northern part of the nation / sold papers to stave off starvation. His feet were cold / inside the church it might be safer. If I see Jesus, Jimmy says, I'll give him a paper.*

Jimmy goes into a church and says Jesus this is Jimmy. Jesus this is Jimmy. It's me. I'm here and you are. Please listen to me. *You might say that was the only way / that little Jimmy knew how to pray.*

The preacher tells Jimmy to leave the church. Out on the streets, he freezes like the

Little Matchgirl. But instead of falling into a vision of warmth and family, he's taken to a hospital where a miracle brings him back to life. *Jimmy, this is Jesus. Jimmy, this is Jesus.*

At the end, Don sings *Rock of Ages* with this bellowing voice that slides right past the notes or never reaches them. But he sings with passion, with innocence and trust.

He's good, I say to Frances, and she pats my arm. There now honey, he always does that. He heard it on the radio.

There's a woman right behind me in a shiny deep-blue home-sewn blouse. It's the color and brilliance of Christmas foil or the eyes of tin Christmas angels. It's shimmered behind me the whole evening. Now and then I've caught her eye, hoping to see her smile. Merle is the only one smiling here, and it seems odd, almost out of place, like a color photograph from one of our late-twentieth-century vacations—dad smiling in the pool, dad smiling with the giant marlin, dad smiling with a piña colada and mom beside him—placed down in the middle of nineteenth-century seriousness.

When Don's finished, he calls the woman up to sing. Her husband comes with her, dressed in bright yellow like a parrot. He has a white mustache and hair, smooth skin.

They walk to the front of the church. Sweet hour of prayer, they tell Edna, and she begins to play. *He walks with me and he talks with me and tells me I am his own.*

They sing with such a deep humility, or shyness, or fear—or trust—that they turn, slowly, away from the congregation until they face the wall. It's like they're turning away from, or into, some great wind. We can only see their faces reflected in the bubbled windows.

There are different ways to live with gloom. One way is to rest in it, to feel the waves of it like a boat on top of water. Another is to sink down into the weedy dark and brood. And another is to fly above it all like a whirlwind, white and swirling, funnel-shaped (and you inside where it's beautiful and wild, like some romantic leaning out over a deep gorge to feel the whirling).

In the daylight, you can see Merle's house and the bare field waiting for some new enthusiasm. Across the street there's a concrete wall. Trucks drive out from the factories, and empty drums of black sludge behind it, out here in the country where no one's supposed to care.

And all up and down Merle's road, on every front porch and front-yard tree, you can see the spinning. All the cast-off, transcendent plastic bottles—spinning whirligigs in the winter air.

nineveh

*Who can tell if God will turn
and repent, and turn away from
his fierce anger, that we perish
not?*

—The Book of Jonah

i

Three of us are standing in the hallway, cataloging frightening things. There's a hole in the ozone over New England that's growing faster than even the worst prediction. There are the droughts, the floods, the way it never gets cold enough anymore for the ponds to freeze in winter, the April snows when the flakes were as thick as bread. The way the grass used to teem with tree toads and grasshoppers, how rare it is to see them now. The way that, on a spring-like February day, you can't rejoice, something in you saying *too soon, too soon*.

But what really scares me, my friend Jim says, is that nerve gas buried all over the place in rusting canisters. There's supposed to be a lot of it, I mean a lot of it, down at Camp Atterbury.

My husband's father grew up, I tell him, in the middle of Atterbury. They lived on a farm just outside of Nineveh, in a town called Kansas. Nineveh was spared when the army built the camp, but Kansas was blown off the face of the earth. The place his house used to be is in the middle of a target range now.

Every year on Memorial Day they open up the off-limits part of the camp so that all the descendants of Kansas can drive through.

The last time we went was the year of the locust plague, when even the insects made a whistling bombing sound. The ground in parts of Atterbury was so pockmarked it looked like the moon.

People sitting in their offices hear us talking. Someone cries out with an exaggerated moan, and the others join in. You gloomy people, they say, you gloomy gloomy people. Cut it out right now; we won't hear any more of it.

The first drought summer made a stir. There was a kind of thrill, like a bad accident. Maybe this is the end of the world, we said, but no one really believed it. It was a pornographic, manufactured thrill, a soothing quick flash of horror, a tear in the fabric of illusions that holds us, more or less comfortably, in mid-air. My town is safe, my neighborhood and house. Everyone lives the way I do, and if they don't, they should. I'm a nice person, so I can't do any harm. I won't live through a depression or a plague or war in my back yard. I'll never be in a concentration camp. I'll never be in a falling airplane. There will never be another nuclear explosion. I will never ever die.

That first hazy drought summer I spent an hour each Monday afternoon talking to a friend who brought her van-load of four children to the piano teacher who lived across the street from me. It was the only time during the week that I could talk to her. She works as a pharmacist all weekend and all week long she lives in the van, driving the children to lessons. There is never a day for her that isn't ordered. The chaos of that large family is tempered by that order. Like music, she creates a rhythm, a form to weave their lives around. Because at times the heart, the world, seems filled with humming cells, like wasps you think, and you think chaos, and every thought turns to containment, separation, to building nests dark as a whirlpool, as a storm.

The piano teacher's husband left several years ago. Now and then we would see him pulling in the driveway, dressed in jeans, to take one of their two boys deer hunting. The teacher was Mormon, and one of her sons did mission work for a year in South America. The other boy collected guns. The boy who collected guns spent hours teaching the neighborhood children how to make whistles from grass blades, how to make maple-seed helicopters spin. Who can explain it?

Anyway, my friend's brother-in-law works for the EPA. Two or three times a year the government flies him to Antarctica to look at the tear in the ozone there. One year when he visited, I saw him look hopelessly at his crying daughter. If you were a lake, he said, I could fix you.

He's at a conference in Canada, my friend said. Has he talked to you about this drought? I asked her. The grass was dry and rough, the children red with heat. My baby girl was in the open van, asleep. She sighed this deep sigh. She was two years old then, and her tongue still made that rhythmic clicking nursing sound against the palate, the one that babies make when they sleep.

He said that it's all over. Everything on this earth is ruined, and there's nothing we can do to reverse it.

When the lessons were finished for the day, I held my sleeping daughter and watched the van drive off. All around, the oak trees were in crisis. Soon the ground would be bumpy with acorns; the squirrels would be building their nests high up off the ground.

When the third drought summer came, we didn't comment. We watered our roses and our pets and our children. We didn't comment. That's how deep the fear had burrowed in.

i i

Sunday morning, 5 A.M., and my daughter gets a sliver of fingernail caught in her blanket's satin binding. She cries and holds her hand and blanket out for me to see and to uncouple, like she's holding the skirt of a ball gown, her eyes glossy with sleep.

I disconnect her and then stand fully awake while she drifts back under. I'm the only one awake in this fragile boat, this rocking house.

Sunday morning, 5 A.M., and I decide to drive to Nineveh. For a week I've been obsessed with it.

Nineveh. Some mythic place. The town that was spared.

The gas station's as bright as a spaceship or a carnival. I fill the car with gas then go inside to pay and ask to see a map. The boy inside is happy to see another human being; he offers to fill my cup with coffee, takes out a map, and we look for Nineveh. Camp Atterbury is map-defined, perfectly rationalized, straight-lined. But in the top left-hand corner there's a notch cut into the camp, and a dot for the town. There's nothing that shows where Kansas used to be.

Once you get outside of Franklin, on the map at least, the roads to Nineveh disappear. I'm sure you'll see a sign, he says, and he asks me what I think I'll find there. I have no idea, I say, and I tell him I'm working on a story about the towns outside the fort.

What do I know about the place? I know my father-in-law came home one day from Nineveh High School and said he hated it, that all he wanted from his life was to be allowed to farm. He never went back to school. But then the farm was seized, and the family moved, and it was like one world had ended and been replaced by another.

It was World War II. Things happened quickly. It was just a matter of days between the government's order to vacate and the day the families had to leave. These were families that had lived there since the early 1800s. It was harvest time. People were angry and confused; they worked day and night, hauling their worldly goods out in trucks. Why here? Why

Kansas and not Shelbyville? Why Kansas and not Bloomington or Spencer or Evansville? Why not Nineveh?

It was confusing, chaotic, the rules constantly changing. A family wanted to take a garage they'd just built with them to their new home. The army said no, they might need it, and then they bulldozed it down. Families with orchards weren't allowed to come back to their land and pick the apples. Government property, they were told, you're in violation of the law. Another family owned a sawmill. They had about 10,000 board-feet of cherry lumber laying out seasoning when the government told them they had so many days to move it. They couldn't get enough trucks, and when the time was up, the soldiers poured gas on the wood and burned it. The army came in with tanks and they knocked down the houses and barns. The fields filled with shells.

A lot of the men were drafted, or they went to work in wartime factories outside of the county. A lot of the old people died. There was a war, you couldn't complain too much, but the farmers didn't get enough money from the government to buy other farms, and most of them felt that the land had been stolen from them.

The families were told that they could buy their farms back after the war. And of course that never happened.

My father-in-law was drafted. His father committed suicide. My father-in-law is the world's gentlest, kindest man, but there's sometimes a sadness in him, and in my husband, that seems not entirely their own. It's a sadness that I only notice when it's missing — when I see them chopping wood, say, or digging potatoes — and it feels like a kind of exile. And I want to trace it back to this particular loss.

And I know the army ended up building a town where the farm had been; they called it Tojoburg. It was two rows of storefronts and dummies that appeared and disappeared from windows like giant puppets. There was a fake cemetery with a large tombstone that said Hitler. The whole place was filled with smoke bombs. They used Tojoburg to practice capturing a town.

Good luck, the boy says, and I put my hand in my coat pocket, looking for change to buy the map. I pull out a handful of coins mixed in with gold and silver stars from one of my daughter's hair ornaments. For weeks, every time I've looked for my keys or gotten in or out of the car or reached to buy something, stars have fallen on the ground like dust. It takes us both a minute to separate them.

I drive on back roads in the dark. Every few miles there's a small cluster of fragile trailers, the neon red-and-blue flash of Pepsi and Coke machines, a brooding church.

There's a pink motel in Amity called Desperation Depot. I turn south, toward Atterbury, just as the sun begins to rise.

Entrance, the sign says, *Camp Atterbury. The State of Indiana and US Army will not be responsible for accidents incurred on this road.* I wonder what that means. Land mines? Drunk soldiers? *Fog area. POW Chapel* the next sign says, with an arrow pointing onto a gravel road.

I turn. A mile or two down the road there's a pond. Arch Lake, the sign says.

It's an eerie lake: a gunmetal grayish-blue with white skeletal tops of dead sycamores projecting fifteen to twenty feet above the water, like something out of Dante, some Hoosier version of hell. In a field by the lake I see a man taking a rifle out of a pickup. Permit Only Hunting, a sign says. The man is wearing black sunglasses. There's some kind of an animal in a trap in the flatbed of his truck.

The chapel sits across from the lake like something made with sugar cubes or a child's blocks. It's tiny, a blinding white stucco, with a small cross cut into the east and west walls. The front of the building is glass. And behind the glass, inside the chapel, all the walls are covered with brilliant blue-and-yellow murals of Mary and St. Anthony and the Dove of

Peace and greeting-card angels. All the figures have halos of light that are reflected, oddly, on the tops of their heads, like their corporeal selves are turning to light, fading away. The altar is painted to look like marble, the floor painted to look like carpet. The eye of God is painted on the ceiling.

The chapel was built by Italian prisoners of war out of cast-offs from other projects. They mixed the dyes from berries, plants, and flower petals. They used their own blood.

The chapel was dedicated in 1943. Just one year before, the churches of Kansas had been destroyed. They exist, now, only in black-and-white photographs.

Most of the camp is still off limits for civilians. There's this corner that's a game preserve, farther in a Job Corps center and minimum-security prison. Army reserves still train here. On the weekends, there are often convoys of army vehicles driving down from Indianapolis.

I wonder if the families would come back. They have other lives now, are tied to other places. The children have ranged far across the country. The shift from peace to war happens quickly. The shift from war back to peace happens more slowly, and will never happen if it doesn't happen first in the imagination.

There's an old graveyard down the road from the chapel, and I stop there, looking for familiar names. The stones are those thin, bread-shaped ones, many of them leaning or shattered, the names mostly illegible. Most of the stones are close to 200 years old. One stone is wedged underneath a dead tree stump. The tree was probably a sapling when the grave was made right next to it. For shade, the family probably thought, protection for my son / father / husband.

I hear a whistle in the background, a man screaming orders. I think of those canisters of nerve gas. I think of unexploded shells.

Someone has, just recently, used Global Van Lines tape to affix a plastic flower to every stone in the graveyard. I have no idea why.

i i i

Nineveh is laid waste: who will bemoan her? Whence shall I seek comforters for thee?

—The Book of Nahum

Nineveh. The first thing you see is an abandoned brick school in that heavy federalist style like Carnegie libraries. *Nineveh School* is carved in stone above the door; it's the same light stone as a gravemarker. Shredded black shades blow against the jagged windows. The ground is covered with broken glass and asphalt tiles.

Two men are loading scrap wood and bricks into the back of a pickup, like ants dismantling a picnic; little by little, the school will disappear. In the basement of the school, there's a green chalkboard with yellow lines, spray painted with graffiti, and a chair facing an open window. There are half-hearted boards over a couple of windows, a piece of wood hanging precariously above my head when I look in the front door, the spooky cooing of doves.

I get back in the car and drive through town. Nineveh Square, American Dream Realty. There's an old stone building built into the side of a hill; there'd been a fire, the inside blackened like a kiln, only the husk of stone. Three speedboats with broken windshields lie in a field next to a pole barn, next to the black lace of a satellite dish.

And all along the east and south edges of the town there are white signs and metal fencing. US Army, No Trespassing. The town is wedged into the army base; it leans against it like a child resting against his father. There's an old white farmhouse in the very corner of town with the army signs nailed to the side and backyard trees, and in front of the house a clothesline hung with handmade afghans, a green ceramic goose with a red bonnet.

I stop at a combination restaurant/grocery store/gas station/sporting goods/video shop. Bait, tackle, ammunition, gift cards. A large box of live crickets alongside a display case filled with guns, and beside that boxes filled with tangled nests of fish hooks, rows of bright orange vests. A stuffed boar's head on one wall, a deer on another, a fox on a third. A stuffed bass curves toward the ceiling with its mouth in a large O.

And walking in and out the doors, lounging in booths, and standing in line at the checkout, there are soldiers. Boys, all of them, in their late teens, early twenties. They're dressed in green camouflage, like mottled surgical scrubs.

In between the restaurant and grocery there are two—legal or illegal?—slot machines called *Motherlode*. There's a glass front on the machines where you can see a bar sweeping back and forth over a mass of quarters. They somehow clump together, and there's an edge where some of the quarters dangle precariously. You get to keep the quarters that fall over the edge; but you have to put your own quarters in to change the balance.

I watch while a group of soldiers stands at each machine, shattering dollars into quarters and throwing them in, one after another. One boy throws away fifteen or twenty dollars. He gets back $1.50, maybe two dollars. This is my coke money, one boy says, my video rental, says another, my eggs and bacon, says a third, and still, they can't stop throwing it away. That's what I get, one boy says after he loses all his quarters, for gambling on a Sunday.

Nineveh is the town that Jonah was running from when he was swallowed by the whale. Go tell those wicked Ninevites I'm going to destroy them, God says, and Jonah runs hell-bent the other way, trying to ignore God's voice. It doesn't work. He goes to sea and God sends a tempest and Jonah's sucked down into the darkness of the whale. *The waters compassed me about, even to the soul,* he says. *The depths closed me round about, the weeds were wrapped about my head.*

The cuneiform for the word *Nineveh* is a fish within a box, the mirror image of Jonah in the whale in just the way that the word *Nineveh* is the mirror image of *heaven*. After several days he's resurrected, back on land with the spirit of the fish inside of him.

And he runs to Nineveh. And he warns them to change their ways. And miraculously they do. Even the king puts on sackcloth and goes down into the ashes and asks to be forgiven. And God, the swimming god, god of the whale, forgives them.

And Jonah sulks. Jonah pouts. I knew you'd do this, he says, softhearted God. I knew you'd make me look like a fool.

He goes up on a hill outside the city and sits in the sun. God makes a surreal gourd appear above his head to cool him; then two days later He takes it away. Two books of the Bible later, Nineveh is destroyed, and the whole Book of Nahum gloats over it. "And there is a multitude of slain," the writer says, "and a great number of carcasses; and there is none end of their corpses; they stumble upon their corpses. Behold I am against thee, saith the Lord of hosts. . . . I will cast abominable filth upon thee, and make thee vile." I asked a theologian why this book's so angry. The people of Nineveh were Assyrians, he said, the enemy. They had wealth and power, and culture. The clay tablets of the *Epic of Gilgamesh* were found there with one of the earliest versions of an apocalyptic flood. In the Book of Luke, Christ, in an apocalyptic mood, says that he is to the world as Jonah was to Nineveh, that there will come a day so painful that we will ask the mountains to fall down on us, a day when we will ask to be covered by the hills.

The ground in the Nineveh cemetery is hard and bumpy. It creaks when you walk on it, like a partly frozen lake.

There are a lot of soldiers' graves. Lee

Park, Spec 4 US Army. Donald Ramey, Sgt. US Air Force, Korea, Retired. Rodney Thompson, another Spec 4, General Supply Company, thirty-three years old when he died. His parents' stone is right next to his, with the date of their marriage and no other dates. Their son's grave is a fresh one.

All around me love is fixed like that, a cup held under a fountain of light, freeze-framed, lovely as glass. A woman who died in 1991, only twenty-eight years old. Her heart-shaped stone a record of her husband's grief. *Wife,* the stone says, and there's an etched rose and a cross, and *The Lord Is My Shepherd*. And John McKee, who died in 1980. *The Hours Part Us, his gravestone reads, But They Bring Us Together Again*. His wife Patsy's name on the stone, only forty years old when her husband died. *The Hours Part Us But They Bring Us Together*. The words, even the stones themselves, assume duration—in love, in the natural world, in the soul—and it's a duration that stands solid in the face of the cup that always shatters, the hill that always slides into the river, the peace that turns to war, the body that always dies. This world is the place where the price of duration is sadness, the note held to the point where the throat aches.

I've never heard anyone talk about the rural families that were uprooted during the war. No one I've mentioned it to remembers it. Even in my husband's family, they scarcely ever talk about it, and most of the information I have comes from a book of oral histories I happened across. The family doesn't talk about it in the same way that a lot of the men who served in World War II, or any war, don't talk about it. It feels like a collective amnesia, though I think it comes from the human tendency to want to protect your children from even the knowledge of your own pain and your own tragedies.

But of course children know there's something there. And they take on their parents' pain as their own painful mystery.

When Kansas was moved, they also moved the graveyards. Fifteen cemeteries containing 1,500 graves. Rich, rolling farmland. Schools and churches. Fifteen hundred graves. In some families, there were over six generations of the living and the dead.

j u b i l e e

*"Nothing matters, and
what if it did?"*

—John Mellencamp

We spent the summer looking for John Cougar.

I don't know what I'd do if I saw John Cougar, I say to Jack. I think I'd die.

We'll see him, Jack says to me, by the end of the summer. We'll make it a hobby to search. Why not? John Cougar moved back here from some place glitzy. We listen to his songs to see how we're doing, like doctors with a stethoscope listening to our own hearts.

John Cougar wants to see us, he says, as much as we want to see him.

Jack unwraps the new tape exactly like a pack of cigarettes. He puts it into the deck. They say you can see him sometimes in the drugstore. We drive by. There's one old pharmacist, no John Cougar.

Oh, I can think of John Cougar and glide. His hair as brown as maples. His voice a night-time field of dry beans, husk on husk.

We drive around two hours with the windows open, listening to John Cougar's voice, hoping to see him on the back roads.

We tell each other secondhand stories about his house. A family farm, with rooms added on. A studio in the barn. I read in a magazine that there's a room for watching movies, a full-size screen. I imagine him singing as he climbs over fences. I see it in slow motion, like a cowboy movie. He has this sort of sad look like he knows things and has come home. It makes me feel good to know I never left.

Now and then we think we see him, and we speed up. But it's never him.

Will you always love me? I ask Jack.

There are some questions you can't answer, he says, and shouldn't try.

Like how we could live ten miles away from someone like John Cougar and be the only people in town who haven't seen him.

At any moment we might see him, I say, riding his bike on the road, hear his real voice, his knock at the door, asking to borrow a cup of something, like any neighbor.

It was a strange year. It was like all your life you'd counted on things and then you couldn't. In the spring there was this plague of locusts. They coated the tree branches. There was this ringing sound all day like bells, it wasn't pleasant. Sometimes they'd all rise and then squeal down like bombs in old movies. They left their dried shells on the ground, and when you walked outside they flew in your face.

Then there was the ice storm. It was beautiful, every bit like diamonds. But all the wires snapped and even some of the old oak trees were uprooted. And that April snow where the flakes were so thick they looked like slices of Colonial.

Two of my friends had miscarriages when the corn tasseled.

And then the summer, no rain for three months. It made you want to stop thinking. It made you want to look for John Cougar. We spent the summer looking for John Cougar, and we would have headed on right through the fall.

But in August, there's this sale on cars, in town where the buildings are falling in. The dealer is moving to the strip by the highway. So he puts up flags and colored lights like a garage sale. Someone sets up a corndog trailer, Polish sausage with peppers, and lemonade. It's the last business to leave from that block. Everyone else had left, a couple of bars moved in, but they strike like a match and just as soon fade.

For a few weeks there's this festival feeling. In the center of the lot is a tent with white lights beading the edge. Underneath it is a new white car. They are going to have this contest. The contest is why we stopped looking for John Cougar. Jack stands outside the tent, his eyes filled with that car.

It's one of those nights I look at him and I know how young we are. He's tall, but his body is a boy's. I want to touch him, but he won't have it, not here. He moves away from the tent and sits on a stack of tires, waiting with his friends. They put on these James Dean faces. The strip of grass on the road is dry and white.

Jack spent the last week waxing our old car so he can sell it when the new one comes. He has faith.

The dealer motions to the boys on the tire. He picks up a big bullhorn and announces that it's time for the New Car Jubilee. Thirty or so men come forward, a few women. They all lay their hands on the car like something holy. A few of the men who weren't as fast are kneeling on the ground, their hands on a hubcap or a fender. The dealer takes all their names. They'll keep their hands on the car for days. If they lift them off at any time but the scheduled breaks, they're out of the contest. The last one holding on will win. The white car, it glistens on their faces.

Jack's wedged in sideways but has a good spot in the center. He can lean on the roof without bending. He's pressed his body tight against the car so no one can get underneath and make him lose his balance. He looks at me and smiles. This is it, the look says, our life is starting. Watch out John Cougar. Last year the winner stuck it out for three weeks. He's cleared it with his boss. They say they'll hold his job until the day he sails into the parking lot in that big white car.

The wives and girlfriends stand outside the circle of the tent. We're ready with pillows and thermos jugs of coffee, home-baked pies and sandwiches. During the breaks, some of the wives are as smooth and well-trained as pit crews.

He's brought a lawn chair for me and set it up where I can watch him. The night is close. The plastic webbing sticks to my skin.

Several men drop out, laughing, within the first hour. They make jokes about why they're leaving. They laugh too loud, wish the others well. The bars across the street are filled with yellow light. Hours pass and after each break there are fewer bodies touching the car, someone lying stretched out on a sleeping bag saying Oh God I can't do it, this feels so good.

I stay through the night. I talk to him and wipe his face with cool water. He tells me to go home during the hot part of the afternoons. I leave him with a thermos of shaved ice. My dreams are busy, full of lakes and water.

After the first day, only the committed are left. There are eleven of them. We went to high school with several. There are a few older than us, not many. For most of them, this is the only way they'll ever have a new car. That's probably true for us, though my husband is convinced he will someday have the money.

One of the men ran for mayor in the last election. Like that, this is something to do with his time. He talks to everyone now, has that politician's smile. He acts like he knows things. He has five children. His wife lives in a van, driving them to lessons. He wears a regular cloth shirt with a button-down collar. Everyone else wears t-shirts. When the talk turns to the weather, he smiles. Oh yes, he says, it's the end, it's all over. Everything's ruined. But me and my husband, we're just starting, I say. He waves his hand, no matter.

The other men laugh and say come on, if that were true, we'd see it on television.

Twice a day his wife drives by and brings him food. He waves to his children through the van windows before they drive off.

No one thinks the contest will last as long as last year's because of the heat. But days pass. Some nights it's quiet on the lot, some rowdy. When the nights are cooler, and on the weekend, it seems like everyone in town shows up. I get tired from all the talk. In the middle of the night men stumble out of the bars and have slurred conversations with those holding onto the car. Their voices begin to slur as well. They start to look pale, like this is something they wish they hadn't started. One night the politician passes out, and an ambulance is called to take him home.

I read in the paper that John Cougar is giving a concert at the fair, in the city, an hour away. The day of the concert I go to the grocery in the afternoon. I make a special dinner and pack it in an old basket I find in the garage. I line the basket with a soft blue cloth and put another cloth over it like a pie. I spend a lot of time on it, making it right.

The lot is quiet when I go there at night. There are only six men left. They all look drowsy, leaning on pillows. None of them are talking. They've told their life stories, every joke they've ever heard. One man sits on the ground, his arms wrapped around the fender. I put my hand on my husband's arm. He jumps when I touch him. His eyes look glossy. His face is flushed, his white shirt wet and transparent as a boiled onion.

He tells me this crazy dream he had, about all our bodies breaking apart into glitter like Star Trek, our spirits turning into rainbows and shooting into the sky. I put my hand on his forehead. It feels clammy. Don't you see, he says, we're snared in a difficult time.

One of the wives looks over at me from where she's been giving her husband water. He's hallucinating, she says, delirious. It's been happening to all of them.

It's all energy, Jack says, nothing is real.

It's the old endtimes thing, another woman says. They should call this whole thing off, give them all a car to drive around in for a couple of weeks. It's too hot for this.

Jack is looking at me like he thinks I'll fly apart. Shh, I say. I start humming.

You're hungry, I tell him. I give him food. I give him chicken, a chunk of cheese, a glass of cold, sugared tea. I feed him cherry cake and chocolate cookies. I buy him popcorn from the stand. Nothing fills him up.

At eight o'clock the sky turns milky hazy blue, the sun red and close. The lights come on in the lot. The stars are hidden behind a haze.

I look around. Everything seems shabby. The concrete is cracked and laced with spiky weeds, windows covered with grime. A brick wall that used to be one side of a furniture store has fallen in and no one has bothered to fix it. The sidewalk in front of the store is embedded with purple quartz. Most of the pieces are missing. No one walks over it now without trying to kick another one loose. The air smells like burned grease.

An hour before the concert, there's a breeze. The bar across the street opens its doors to let in the air. They're playing one of John Cougar's songs, distant and tinny. The men around the car try to sing along.

We hear this roaring. Dust rises in the street. I see a tired face in the window of the bar. God damn, someone shouts, it's sure enough him.

John Cougar! John Cougar! we all yell, just like that. We run out to the street and cheer.

Forty thousand waiting to hear him sing, the Midway lit up like Popsicles. Part of me wants to race him to the city, demand he look at me, and tell me what he knows. Part of me sinks close to the earth's spin, still believing he'll see me in his own good time.

We head on back to the car lot. The six men are holding onto the car for dear life. Tell us about it, one of them says, tell us what you saw.

hey john, won't you write a song about my sister stella?

small town

*I see a few people that I
know, family, friends.
I never go out. I sit in
my kitchen, drink tea,
smoke cigarettes, and
talk about the world.*

*The reality is I wouldn't
want to live anyplace
else.**

*The quotations under "Small Town" and "Whenever We
Wanted" are from "The Rolling Stone Interviews: John Cougar
Mellencamp," Rolling Stone, January 30, 1986. All other
quotations are from "John Mellencamp's Melancholy Jubilee,"
Rolling Stone, October 8, 1987.

On the day the Elvis stamps go on sale, an exhibit of John Mellencamp's paintings opens at the Southern Indiana Center for the Arts, in an old house that belonged to one of his childhood friends. In downtown Seymour the Christmas loudspeakers are playing Elvis songs with that hollow sound that outdoor speakers make.

An old man in a black mesh hat, overalls, and a work shirt with an oil stain walks into a hardware store. There's a dusty, yellow-leafed philodendron in the window. In the coffee shop, youngish gray-haired women meet for lunch. The cook dumps a wire basket of fried fish into a metal bin and talks to a waitress about her son. She holds the handle with both hands, bends her whole body to the side and tilts her head as she pours.

There are signs in the dry cleaners that have been up since the sixties, the colors bleaching out and leaving just the words and forms: smiling housewives who look like Jackie Kennedy, their arms around their clean-clothed children. "Fresh as a Flower in Just One Hour." Someone's taken a magic marker and made a homemade sign on poster board and taped it in the window. "There is no sorrow," the sign says, "that Christ can't heal."

There's an amusement arcade next to the dry cleaners that's painted art-deco lavender. It looks like it used to be a theater. The windows are broken out, and there's a cat walking through the empty lobby.

A seamstress does alterations in a store next to a video rental. There are crocheted Barbie ball gowns pinned to cards on a shelf above mountains of human clothes. The sewing machine grinds. A woman in a black cloth coat looks through a box of cast-off shoulder pads for something to put in the blouse she's holding. "I can't seem to get it right," she says. "I came in last week and had them taken out. And I came in today to have them put back in."

In the drugstore they sell John Mellencamp postcards. They keep them in a metal box up near the cashier. "His brother comes in here every day for cigarettes," the cashier tells me. (There are these stories about John's Seymour childhood in the *Rolling Stone* interviews. How, when he was eight, he was put in jail for three hours with all the neighborhood kids for vandalizing a local artist's house. How ironic that seems now. How he told his parents he wrote Donovan's *Universal Soldier*. How weird it is that I know these things about someone I don't even know.)

In the back of the store, the pharmacist talks to one of her customers, a doughy woman sitting in the waiting chair. The woman looks lost. "You know," the pharmacist says, "you shouldn't have run out of that inhaler for a month."

"I spent seven hours at the doctor's in Mooresville," an old man tells the pharmacist's assistant. "And all he talked about was Sunday's ball game. He lectured me then went to lunch then came back and lectured me about the lecture.

"Hardly said anything about the surgery."

A young father stands talking to his seven- or eight-year-old son. "OK now Steven, where are you gonna get the most rebounds? Under the basket? Not at the half-court line screaming I'm open! I'm open!"

I walk outside. The speakers are playing *Jailhouse Rock*. It's a cold, gray day, spitting snow.

I'm here to look at art that's risen from this town, and so I want to see the town as art. I'd like to think that meaning rises constantly from things like carbonation. But it's hard to see that when a place is so familiar. I've lived near here, have relatives just outside the county.

There's a "Proud to Be an American" bumper sticker in the door of Framewerx. On the walls prints of young Victorian girls, children, cats, snow, flowers, an old man praying, horsedrawn carriages, teddy bears with knitted hats, trees in bloom, red sunlit barns, flour mills with symmetrical trees. It's all so pretty.

This is the art we live with, our vision of the good, the way our lives would be if all the pain were boiled away and we were as pure as distilled water. This is the art that calms, the art that reassures.

In the insurance office there are pictures of boys with fishing poles. In the barber shop, a decoupage wooden state of Indiana with a collage of IU basketball players. An old poster: *Aim High—Join the Air Force.*

In the office of the Seymour Monthly, a figurine of an old man with a fish, a macramé plant hanger, a gold-tinted train. Some of John Mellencamp's platinum records hang on the wall (his brother works here) and a sign: To the People of Seymour—Thank you for your support over the past ten years—John Mellencamp.

r . o . c . k . in the u . s . a .

I'm living the dream of a 19 year old boy from Indiana and I'm 37 years old. But what happens when you don't want to be young anymore. When the

fascination of being a young
man has left you.

I don't want to be in this race
anymore because it leads to
nowhere.

When Madonna became a superstar, she moved to Miami Beach. There's an intensely frenetic glitz to Miami Beach—magazine photo shoots and peach and aqua hotels that look like radios and everyone on in-line skates. I was there a week ago, and talked to a man who pulled one of her yellow American Express receipts from his wallet and showed it to me like it was a holy relic, like one of those vials they sold in the Middle Ages with John the Baptist's blood or Christ's fingernails.

When John Mellencamp became a superstar, he moved back to Seymour. Think of the contrast. When Madonna steps outside her house, she steps onto a stage, a city of cartoon glamour and violence. When Michael Jackson steps outside his house, it's into an amusement park. When John Mellencamp steps outside his house, he's right here where *we* are. He went out to test the waters and came back. Makes you feel like maybe you were right to stay.

When I started working on this essay, one

of my good friends asked me who John Mellencamp is. This is an intelligent, well-read woman, a wonderful poet. I said, well, think of superstars you've heard of. Lord Byron. Liszt. Frank Sinatra. People enormously popular in their own time. He's somewhere between those people and the ones who are well-known only in a certain specialized niche — like nuclear physicists. Or contemporary poets. Maybe a notch down from Michael Jackson in name recognition, but equal to Bruce Springsteen. Who? she said.

Anyway, imagine them moving back to the provinces, maybe *this* province, and setting up their studios. And maybe, while they're at it, taking up a second art and pursuing it seriously.

When he started painting, he *studied*. Art history. Technique. He took classes at IU, at the Art League, in New York. For a while he painted in the garage, sometimes more than ten hours a day. Then he built a studio near his house. "It was winter, and there's no heat in the garage," he said. "I'd get the oil on the palette and the fucking oil would freeze."

He's performed for millions of people, turned crowds of thousands into one organism (like what — like coral, like larger bodies out of single cells) and we want to somehow deify him for it, for that transformation, that temporary euphoric escape from our solitary lives.

God, how we love that communal rush. How much we want to glorify the one who gives it to us. How tempting it must be to believe the power is yours. How dangerous it can be. And how hard it must be to refuse the power, to keep your focus on the art itself, away from your own blossoming ego.

w h e n e v e r   w e w a n t e d

I do think that music can change things. But not now. How are we supposed to take you guys seriously when you've got a corporate sponsor underneath your names.

I think you can say much more in a painting than you can in a stupid song.

The first time I see the paintings is the night of the opening. There's a jazz band and valet parking. Some artists down from India-napolis and Columbus, but mostly the crowd is from Seymour — friends of the Mellencamps, doctors, local politicians, people who can afford the $50 charge.

Mellencamp's family is here. His mother and sister look exactly like him—the same beautiful dark eyes and hair.

The opening is festive, warmly lit. It feels comfortable and close, like a church Christmas party. Some of the young artists actually look at the paintings. "What do you think?" I ask a young woman. She's a painter herself, with ethereal blonde hair. "He's very good, and he's only been doing this for four years, imagine it," she says.

"But tell me," she asks, and she turns away from the paintings. "Why all these New Orleans dance hall women? Why are they so miserable? And why does he keep looking at them?" I say something lame and academic about the expressionists liking circus and dance hall themes because they were looking for a revival of spirit. Intensified life. A reaction against bourgeois middle-class materialism, against a deceptively stable society. Rock comes from similar Dionysian impulses, I say, and I'm ashamed of myself for saying it. I think I even mention Nietzsche: Blessed are the despisers, because they are the ones that cross over. I hardly ever talk like this.

"I'm sorry," I say to her. "I'm a teacher."

"That's OK," she says.

I overhear John's mother joking to a friend. They're standing in front of a painting called *Balance*. Where a cartoon man stabs a green-dressed woman with a dagger. There are angles like the German expressionist Kirchner. Skulls balanced against colors, a snake with a crimson tongue, a bare-breasted woman in a bed balanced against a bare-breasted man. The man holds a whip.

"I said John," his mother says, "will you tell me about this painting. 'I was just experimenting with forms and color,' he said, but I said come on John, I'm your mother, you had to be thinking *something*."

"They're so German," another woman says. "So dark. All this death and graveyards."

An older doctor is wearing his weekend beige sweater. "My wife told me not to dress up," he says, "so I didn't." He looks around. "Johnny's done pretty good by himself," he says. Two young women in black stand looking at an almost life-size painting titled *Missy*. "Is that his new wife or his old one?" one asks. "His new one I think," the other says. They look at the lovely face, the woman's red movie-star dress. The folds of fabric so sensual you want to touch them. "Come over here," the first one says, "and look." At a certain angle, the shadows in the face take over, turn into a dark beard and mask. An artist tells me it's because he did or did not use either turpentine or linseed oil to mix the black—I can't remember which.

People seem very kind, unpretentious. Sweet. Everyone smiles, jokes with that self-deprecating midwestern irony. For the most part we politely ignore the paintings like we would a death. These are passionate paintings, and this is the Midwest, where we farm our passions, define their boundaries. It's like basketball (or square dancing, or marriage)—you can jump in all energy and joy, secure in the knowledge that the discipline, the pattern of the game or dance, will hold you. You jump into vacations headlong, knowing that if one weekend flings you onto beaches and hills all yielding languid curves, the next will fling you into orderly lines, back home again to Indiana.

There are some whispers. "He's here," someone says, "John's here." He doesn't seem to enter, just appears. He finds a spot in the back of the house, in front of a painting called *The Babysitter,* a portrait of a large, evil-looking person of indeterminate sex.

He's quiet, modest, polite to the men and women who stand around him. He mostly talks to people older than he is, friends of the family, like you would at a reunion. He's wearing a jacket and blue jeans. He talks about basketball, last weekend's IU game. "Where are your tickets?" someone asks him. He says that he doesn't have regular seats, that he calls the office when he wants to go.

"Are you an IU fan?" someone asks his wife. "I've had to become one," she says. "I'm a Hoosier fan now." She's tall, her blonde hair pulled back tight, no makeup—that off-duty fashion model look where all the beauty's reined in, gathering force. Like one of those 3-d pop-up birthday cards waiting to open up all tropical fruit and glitter and confetti. There are several paintings of her on the walls. "She's the one in the Victoria's Secret catalog," a woman had told me earlier, "the blonde whose eyes they make look oriental." She leans into John, never lets go of him, seems draped across his shoulder, along his arm, like a silver scarf.

John brings up Farm Aid, how many hours Willie Nelson will spend signing autographs. "Hey John," a man asks, "was that your Harley in the movie?" It was. "And your car?" The same. "My nine-year-old asked if she could have the car when she was older. I said sure, if she could tell me what kind of car it was. She could." He smiles when he talks about his daughter, shakes his head like any father.

He says thank you when anyone compliments him on the paintings, but he doesn't want to talk about them, refuses to be interviewed about them. It's all too fragile. Once a young artist in a wheelchair asks him about his palette. The wheelchair is splattered with paint like a cheerful Jackson Pollack—bright crayon colors. "I only use about eight colors," John answers.

After he's been there a half an hour, he looks at his watch and whispers to his wife. It's time to go. "Hey John," a man says as he heads toward the door, "write a song about my sister Stella. You do that, OK?"

l o n e l y   o l '   n i g h t s

I'm the world's worst at relationships. Are you kidding me? I'm retarded. I've been married two times—and both times married to wonderful women—and I've managed to fuck that up somehow. Relationships. Yeah, they'd mean a lot if I knew how to have one. To really relate to a woman—ahh. I don't know how to do it.

It's the first day of sun we've had in

months. The last time I was through here the water that runs through the fields into White River was olive colored and muddy. Today it looks like jewelry.

Today I get to see the paintings in the light, with fewer people around, to really look at them.

But the gallery's more crowded than I expect it to be. "People have been coming from all over. It's been like this constantly," the director of the gallery says.

This is a slightly different crowd. Young Harley biker fathers with their blonde kids and wives dressed in black. Grandmothers in heavy coats. Fraternity boys down from Indianapolis. There are a lot of bare breasts in the paintings, and there's some joking. "Hey this one's me," a woman says, "this is the one he did of me!" and her friends all laugh. "You wish!" one says.

"God, I wish I was a rock star," a frat boy says. "Get to paint all these topless women. Didn't he live for a while with both wives and his kid in Hilton Head? Man, I'd love to be a rock star."

"Hey look at these paintings man," his friend says, motioning to *Balance*. "You think he's happy?"

And that's the response to the paintings, it's hard to see them without thinking about him, about his happiness. He's living the dream, so is he happy? The consensus is that he's not, but then we wouldn't expect him to be. That's part of the myth of success.

"What do you think?" I ask an older woman.

I'm asking about the painting she's looking at but she says "You want to know? He's a troubled man. He is. He's troubled."

"Why do you say that?"

"Because everything's so dark," she says. "I guess you sometimes get the best art from people like that."

"That's not bad," a younger woman says. She points to a portrait called *Rainey*. "It's one of the lightest ones. She doesn't look so tormented there; she looks like a normal person.

"A psychologist would have a field day with these."

"Does he ever come here?" the woman's son asks the director. He's about nine or ten years old, has this innocent, expectant face. "He's been here a few times," she answers him, and the boy says "Wow."

"The poor thing," the mother says, still looking at the paintings, "he seems so unhappy."

"I think he's got a problem," another woman says. "There's a lot of tension, violence. I don't see any love in any of 'em except maybe"—and she points to *Missy*—"except maybe her face."

"You can have these moods," the grand-mother says, and she smiles, "but everything depends on how long you let 'em last.

"And this one's obviously gone on way too long. He needs to pull himself out of it."

"His new wife's real pretty," the young mother says. "Maybe he'll be happy now."

i a i n ' t   n e v e r   s a t i s f i e d

*If an art critic came in and
looked at my paintings he'd
go — Man you are so old-
fashioned and so behind the
times.*

*Sorry — I'm not dying to
be hip.*

*Some days I start at
7 o'clock and I paint until
five, eat dinner and come
back and paint until midnight.
I don't have to talk to anybody.
It's better than sex, for me.*

It's a lifelong commitment,

something I can do in my old
age. It makes life bearable.

The paintings.

It's like he's taken all the pleasant stereo-types, the niceness, down off the walls of the insurance store and the dry cleaners and said see, there's this underneath it.

On the cover of his last CD, *Whenever We Wanted,* there's his beautiful wife sitting on a chair, echoes of the lines in Picasso's *The Guitar Player,* John himself sitting on a chair with his guitar, and between them John's painting *Whenever We Wanted II,* a man and a woman in the same position but this time emaciated, turned away from each other, hollow-eyed, the flesh drooping on the bones like old cloth. There's this, and also this.

Most of the paintings are portraits. There's *Adam and Eve.* Adam's sunken chest, orange-kneed, blunt-toed, Eve's nipples hovering on the breasts, a cigarette in Adam's hand mercurochrome orange, the same orange at the genitals. Eve stands at attention. There's *Stella,* with her drooping breasts, an ocher star in the middle of her face.

Gates of Hell is the largest, most ambitious painting. It's a couple with a child standing at the gates of hell. The woman with a witch's hat shaped like the dagger she's holding in her hand. Lime-green sun shines through the leaves of the holly bush outside the gallery window the day I'm looking at it; there are circles of the same lime-green at the base of the dagger, a cool aqua in the baby's shoes, but the rest of the palette's angry or a swirl of foggy Baudelaire absinthey soupy green. Again, the cigarette-coal orange on the dog's nose, scrotum, fingernails. The dog's white fangs. Lean hounds, all crouching violence. The man's right hand is splayed like a child's drawing of a hand; that's the arm that's holding the baby, three pinkish flamingo halos above the baby's head. The couple is overwhelmed by it all. *Hell, we just did what we did, whenever we wanted to.* It's said that he started painting when he was going through his second divorce.

Balance. The guitarist sits against the wall, skull-like, a rope around his neck attached to the blonde/Indian/Egyptian impassive bare-breasted man's wrist. The woman in the bed is anguished. The woman being stabbed is innocent. A couple stands in the doorway with expressions of false concern.

Your Mother. Holds a leather belt. Her body's anorexic. Her eyes are dead. She wears a shift. Bottle-green legs. Algae-green walls. Her hands are wooden. Her hair is chopped. She holds a leather belt.

Kristi. She's blindfolded. A lot of the women are.

Headgivers. Two women. Masculine like the drag queen babysitter, hints of dark shadowy hair, stick upper arms, sloped shoulders. A red gloved hand like a fist at the crotch. Black holes for eyes.

Party Goers. In the foreground, a hoop of gray chair. Narcissus in a vase, the shadow of the flowers a dark explosion, like reverse fireworks. There are two parents and a child. The child is a devil, dwarfed by the chair. He has an adult mouth, shadowed eyes through a red mask—a deep blood red. (In the other room, a painting called *The Happy Couple*. The man's holding a knife.)

nothing matters and what if it did?

I wonder about Bruce Springsteen's happiness. About Madonna's happiness, and Michael Jackson's. Hey, let's quit feeding off these people.

The woman at the opening was right. It's German. This part of southern Indiana has a lot of German roots. "White Creek

Lutherans," one of my relatives calls her neighbors. I asked a friend of mine, a German historian, if he could say why there's all that darkness in German art. It's a question he wouldn't touch.

"I came to painting through the impressionists," Mellencamp says. "It's sweet, but not real." He saw the paintings of Beckman and other German expressionists and everything opened up for him. And what the expressionists expressed was often a dark vision. And that darkness is what his neighbors notice. Poor Johnny, why is he so sad.

But the expressionists painted passion, the uncontrolled expressed passion of the artist with nothing in between. What he sees outside himself is not as important as the way it affects him. It was feeling, not knowledge. And maybe when you crack open the place where feelings are kept, you crack open first of all the ones that have been caged or denied, the ones that aren't so pretty.

Some of the expressionists, in the 1890s, even glorified war, again because of Nietzsche; let's blow the old away and make way for the new. But that raw force that's creative during times of malaise, the one that first seems to bubble up in adolescence (or in a rock career), can also be destructive, both powerfully renewing and powerfully and indiscriminately dangerous.

So when World War I began, the expressionist artists were at first exhilarated. And then they saw the horror. "Just try painting this," Beckman said, "in an impressionistic style." Their paintings got even darker.

Hitler took the expressionist paintings down from the walls of German galleries because they didn't paint the light and airy rural Aryan vision of the fatherland. It was like Dr. Jekyll and Mr. Hyde, that attempt to split evil from good, to purify "the good." If only the paintings had been allowed to stay up.

One of the things a religious ritual is supposed to do is give us the space for us to come together and look, in a community that gives us the courage to do so, at mystery—whether it's terror at the silent brooding emptiness of space, or earthly decay and violence, or the unutterable joy of grace and love. Art often serves a similar function, folds all the mystery back into the dailiness, back into consciousness. We have to let art do that.

In the United States, expressionism was popular during the Eisenhower era. It rose again during the Reagan years, in the post-apocalyptic vision of the Batman movies and the in-your-face Halloween gore of rock bands like Megadeath. Walk into a record store now and, if you pay attention, you'll be astounded at the split between the vision of the posters on the wall there and the art in all the other stores

surrounding it. This is a legacy of expressionism as well.

I'm not saying that Mellencamp is re-
sponding to a fad. I think he's a much more serious artist than that; over and over in his career he's refused to be co-opted. It's one of the
reasons he moved back here, or that you won't
see ketchup pouring out of a bottle to any of
his songs. But we're all shaped by the culture,
by the times. And we should probably pay attention to what we're saying to ourselves, not
to deny it, or repress it, but to let ourselves see
it and try to understand what it means.

On the way into Seymour on State Road
11 someone's nailed a piece of paper saying
"He is risen!" to a tree. Next to the tree there's
a grape arbor with dried vines draped like
arms. Next to that a sign for homemade noo-
dles, a Pepsi machine leaning against a barn-
wood shed, chickens running across a yard
covered with straw. Mellencamp's parents
home is about a mile away, up a slope from the
Rockford Drive-In. People are always driving
into the parking lot, snapping pictures of his
house, then driving off. "Once I actually saw
John," the carhop told me. "He was nice. He
ordered a Coke." In town, where the Christmas loudspeakers are playing the sainted Elvis,
the tabloids report sightings of him everywhere. There are huge lines at post offices all

over the country, people on pilgrimages to Graceland. This is the United States of America, late twentieth century. We're not sure where to put our faith. We let our old myths shape the new ones.

There's a communal religious feel to rock music; that and sports are the closest a lot of us will ever come to religious fervor. At the end of the concert, you raise your hands and hold a lighted match or lighter. We put an awful lot of faith in rock and roll.

q u a k e

December 3, 1990

It is always the same round, so dull, dull, dull. Nothing happens, nothing, nothing. If only for once something would happen and not leave behind this stale taste of triviality. If only barricades were set up again, I would be the first to take my stand on them. Just to feel the intoxicating enthusiasm, I would welcome a bullet in the heart. Or if a war could just be started up, however unjust a war. This peace is so damned oily and greasy, like a sticky polish on old furniture.

—German poet
Georg Heym, 1910

I'm sitting on a balcony in New Harmony, Indiana, waiting for the end of the world.

I don't mind the wait. Every sixty years the sun and the moon battle for the earth's affections, and the body of the earth turns liquid

and rolls. Earth tides, they're called, and everyone in the Midwest knows about them now.
Something strange and unsettling in the solid
earth we've counted on. We live on one of the
world's largest fault lines, and most of our
lives we weren't even aware of it. Some
prophet named Iben Browning has predicted
that the tide will cause the fault to shift on this
very day, and because we're only ten years
away from the new millennium, something in
us longs for the explosion.

Blow it all up, get rid of it: all the plastic
pens and razors, and the World of Dinettes that
sold us the $100 chairs that fell apart in one
year. Blow up the immense shopping desert
with the acres of stone lots and tall mercury
lights like drooping flowers and all the brand-
new vapory objects that pack the stores so
tightly it makes us dizzy to walk through them.
Blow up the church where we sit without fervor on Sunday, listening to announcements
about the sidewalk fund, and the chaos of strip
malls where it's impossible to walk from Toys
R Us to Children's Palace 100 yards away, and
it takes an hour to drive through a confused
tangle of unplanned traffic lights and road-
ways to the K Mart where last year a five-year-
old girl from my neighborhood reached for a
silver tube of toothpaste on a shelf and it blew
off her hand. I put my own children in a metal

shopping cart now like a cage, and I pray they won't reach their hands outside of it.

Because I've lived in the suburbs of Indianapolis all my life and I remember the forest of 100-year-old beech trees that was cut to make that chaos, and because when I wake up in the middle of the night in the same neighborhood I lived in as a child, the sky isn't dark and crisp and starry, but this weird half-mystical shade of orange-gray-violet, when I heard about the earthquake, I ran hell-bent out of my township, down through the detritus of the city's spinning—past Auto Parts and Used Auto Parts and then old tires submerged in a winter field, past rows of hay huddled under black trash bags. I ran from my own anger, down to where the earthquake map in the paper was shaded, to where I could feel it if it goes. In 1823 a prophet brought a group of people here from Germany to wait for the end of the world. The earthquake, if it comes, won't be just some minor trembling that shakes the curio cabinet here, and the Harmonists who've been waiting first in line, folded into the ground like egg whites for 100 years, will shiver: hush, maybe this is it, what we've been waiting for, new life, our chance to rise. So I sit on a balcony overlooking Paul Tillich's grave, waiting with them for the end of everything.

It doesn't come. I try to meditate on important things. Instead, I think about local gossip, some scandalous reason that Tillich is buried here and the Harmonist granary across the street has never been restored. I think it has something to do with the IU calliope. I can't remember the story, and anyway it's probably not true. I stretch and drink coffee and wonder why I am so shallow even on earthquake day. I put my feet up on the balcony. The day is unseasonably warm, the climate turned strange, the globe a candled egg.

Wild geese rise up from the woods behind the Benedictine chapel. They have difficulty forming a V; one goose moves out in front and then another. The others have no idea which one to follow. Is that a sign? Do geese get confused before earthquakes? Supposedly, cats run away; that's part of the mythology. Keep your eyes on the want ads in the paper. I decide that I need a paper.

I walk downstairs and head toward town, past the log houses, the roofless church. I see the granary behind a gate. Private residence, the sign says. Things like that can't matter when you're waiting for the end of the world, so I walk in.

It's one of the largest barns I've ever seen — stone and log windows, the whole thing shaped like a loaf of bread. It's where the Harmonists stored their hay for the millennium. The barn is covered with dead foliage like tan-

gled hair, two cats sitting in the chink of light
that's opened by a boarded-up window;
maybe they've run away. I try to look inside.
Rotted wood and fallen rafters, an expanse of
dark like a cathedral, dusky light from windows high up. I walk around the corner of the
barn, over to Robert Dale Owen's mad scientist laboratory, a weird Victorian structure
with turrets like witch's caps, a metal fish
twisting overhead. There were two different
utopias here. It was only the first group who
waited for the end of the world. The Owenites
bought the whole town when it didn't happen
and the Harmonists began revising their pre-
dictions. If the Harmonists thought that human beings were angels—Gabriel, it's said,
even left his footprint in a stone above the
Wabash—the Owenites thought they were machines. They were the ones who mapped and
classified every inch of this wilderness, the
ones who brought in the abstract and the rational. Make the perfect world, they thought,
and you create a perfect human being.
Strangely, though, it was the spiritual Harmonists who created the buildings which still stand,
a simple beauty and order in the life they made
much like the Shakers. It was the rational
Owenites who built very little, and when they
did, created this wacky laboratory. Toward the
end of his life, Robert Dale decided the spirit
was so completely disconnected from the body

that he turned to seances, the air in New Harmony so thick with spooky spirits that he
could hardly walk outside.

The wall of the granary on the laboratory
side is covered with trumpet vine, hard dried
bean pods like the beaks of brown yammering
toucans. I break a pod from the vine and put it
in my pocket. The pods shake in the wind and
it sounds like applause; the fish on the laboratory spins and spins.

I leave through the gate and head into
town. I realize that I'll spend the very last day
in the world shopping, the way we celebrate
holidays in the suburbs. Labor Day Sale. Memorial Day Sale. After Thanksgiving, Pre-
Christmas Sale. Armageddon Day Clearance,
everything half-off, take it with you. I try to
talk to people about the earthquake, looking
for a true believer, but only the agnostics are
out.

A woman sits in a bookstore putting all
the change from the church Sunday school into
paper rolls, her finger stuck down inside a roll
like one of those Chinese puzzles. "It's old people and children that are worried," she says to
me, "people who don't have a thing to do. My
mother's boxed up all her stuff and tied the
water heater to the wall with cup hooks. My
little boy's gone to stay with her; they can be
scared together all day long."

A clerk with dangling paper-clippy-looking earrings overhears us. "It's not just old people," she says. "My insurance agent boxed all his stuff up and spent the night in his motor home. I'd be afraid the thing would topple over."

I tell her I talked to an insurance agent before I came down here, one from Anderson who had to hire three extra people to write up earthquake riders on policies even though Anderson's supposedly on a different plate. "You're as safe from this fault in Anderson," I say, "as you would be in Paris."

I buy books for my kids and a newspaper, head out the door. I check the sky, feel my feet on the sidewalk. Is that a rumble? Is everything solid? I put my hand on the cold stone building.

Around the corner to a white house where they sell woven goods. I walk in. Cross-stitch pictures of lambs and bins of colored yarn; maybe I can find a scarf for my brother. He can wear it in January if the weather turns cold enough. January? Yes, I think. January. If I really believed in this prediction, I wouldn't be here. I would have gathered up everyone I love and headed for an open field.

An old woman with short, bowl-cut gray hair sits behind a floor loom. National Public Radio is on louder than any rock station.

Something crashing and dissonant, the wood loom clacks like the dried trumpet vine on the granary.

"I'm not afraid of no earthquake," she says. "You talk about Kentuckians," she says, "but we're ignorant here, that's all. Hoosiers—damn ignorant"—clack crash, the loom, the radio's percussion.

I try a purple shawl on over my coat, and it turns me into an old woman immediately. Last night in the restaurant, two old women with rounded backs, their eyes inches away from the tablecloth when they sat down; they looked like the handles of two umbrellas hooked over the table's edge. I pull the shawl around me, turn away from the mirror. I'm trying on old age to see how it feels.

"Ignorant," the woman says, "because they've never been out of the state in their lives"—clack crash—"never farther than Evansville, some of them, like my son's wife, they're divorced now, I wouldn't have said ignorant while she was married to him, but the week my son wanted to take her on a vacation to Dallas, my ignorant daughter-in-law said it was too far away, and that was the week she moved out with the baby and the furniture."

"Ignorant"—clack crash—"just damn ignorant."

Another old woman in jeans and a red stocking cap comes in the back door, puts down a sack. There are three of us now. I hunch over, move toward the loom.

"We get the baby every eight days," the weaver says, "and they're beating her."

"Who's they?" the woman in the red cap asks.

"How awful," I say.

"They're beating her"—clack crash—"and we can't prove it."

"Scars are being formed there," the other woman says.

"Every eight days then Wednesday Thursday Friday Saturday Sunday, and the baby cries when we try to take her back to her mother."

"Pillar to post," the other woman says, "lifetime scars are being formed there."

The weaver slams the shuttle through the loom. "We don't know who's beating her, she says, maybe the day care, we can't prove it."

"Are there bruises?" the other woman asks.

"No," the weaver says, "but she cries too hard for no reason."

"Scars you can't see," the other woman says, "scars being formed there."

I put the shawl back on the wire and straighten my back.

"I've been to Hawaii," the weaver says, "to my sister's house in California. An earthquake in California, they just look up and go on, not like here."

"Something needs to shake us up," she says.

"Shake rattle and roll," her friend says.

"You like the shawl?" the weaver says to me. "I didn't mean," she says, with a crash, the beater bar shoving the threads so tight they will never unravel, "to tell you a horror story on earthquake day."

I walk outside. Everything is still the way it was, but different. There are earthquake stories everywhere. I walk down the street to the Main Street Cafe, walk in, sit down. Three more old women in a booth next to mine. A man in a John Deere hat walks by. There are all these tired graying faces, but this man's face is a candle. "There were tremors," he says to the table of women, "tremors at 10:30." Of course! Everyone nods, revisionist history. So that's what it was, we think, the sound I heard—not a truck going by on the highway, not a man moving furniture in the apartment upstairs, not a woman taking out her troubles on a loom. It wasn't one of my spells, I hear a woman saying to a friend, right about then it was I leaned into the truck and started hoping that someone would come along and save me. Tremors! Our new lives can begin now, all fresh, everything bad sloughed off like water through a colander.

"You from around here?" one of the women at the booth says to me, just like you would expect her to. "No," I say, "I'm staying at the inn." She tells me she lives in the green stucco house across the street, the one with the ceramic elves in the window, sure that I noticed it. I assure her that I did notice it, and I tell myself I'll look for it when I leave. The last day in the world, and I've become a liar and a trespasser and a thief. There's no hope for me, none whatsoever. The woman is getting ready to go home and watch *Days of Our Lives*. I tell her I haven't liked it much since Doug and Julie left, and Bo and Hope, and she says yeah, that Patch just got killed too, and I tell her I'm sorry, I didn't know.

"Remember when Patch was a bad guy?" I ask. And she says yes, that he was one of those good-looking bad guys that all the viewers fall in love with, so they turned him into a good guy, little by little. But not too good; he still had a wicked edge to him. It would come out when you least expected it. He died a good guy death though, a hero.

I ask what's happening now—gossip, shopping, and soap operas are how we spend the last days of our own real lives—and she says they're all on an island and there's been an earthquake. They're holed up together in a building.

Not on earthquake day, I say to her, and she laughs and says "You're not one of those who believes in earthquakes" as though it's something you need to have faith in, like God or love. And I laugh, say no, I'm not one of those. All of us out to lunch on this day are the ones who don't believe the earth is waiting to swallow us whole for our sins.

One of the woman's friends who lives up near Gary got in with a cult who moved into a church basement a few years ago, believing someone who said there was going to be a killer tornado. She thinks that all these earthquake believers are just as crazy. She tells me about another friend who's rigged up an outdoor generator and put a change of clothes and bottled water in both of her cars, with plans to live in whichever one survives the quake. The woman and her husband are both excited about it; it's given them something to talk about for months.

"I haven't done a thing to get ready for this earthquake," another woman says, as though it's something you have to prepare for, like Christmas.

"If I put all my food in one place," she says to me, "that's exactly the place the wall would cave in."

"You watch soap operas," I say to the women. "When a woman boxes up the baby and the furniture and moves away, what happens?"

"It depends," the ceramic elf woman says. "Sometimes the woman is happier, sometimes not. Sometimes the man is happier than the woman."

"And the baby?" I ask.

"Sometimes an accident," she says.

"Fire, drowning, hurricane, explosion," another woman says. "If the baby survives, she's moved all over the place. Everyone fights over her."

"Babies in soap operas never stay in one place long."

"Sometimes there's a kidnapping."

"Yes!" A woman in her husband's green thermal coat. "Some guy you've never even seen before comes in, claims he's the father and grabs her. Some old lover of the wife—a Mafia guy sometimes, leader of a Virgin Islands cult."

"Everyone comes back together to save the baby," the elf woman says. "The baby's parents fall in love again.

"Months later there's a big wedding, a dress like Lady Di's. We all stay home to watch it, and we cry and cry."

The thermal-coated woman says "And at the last minute, the bride's brother runs in, his clothes all torn and dirty, holding the baby."

"The bride's brother or the groom's best friend."

"No, the guy the bride left her husband for."

Yes, they agree, that's best. And then?

"Bliss," one woman says. She wraps both

hands around her bubbling Coke. "Bliss and bliss and bliss."

"For about a half a year," the elf woman says. "A half a year, then boom, crash, something happens to them. Or they go away for a while and the baby comes back replaced by a teen-age actress and the whole thing starts all over."

"And in real life?" I ask.

"Who knows?" they say. Things happen, they agree, you can't predict. Things just go on and on and every once in a while there's an earthquake. The next day the sun comes up, you look around, and you see whether you're living your old life or a new one. It's exactly what I was afraid they'd say.

The problem with this world is that things are so enmeshed. You can't predict a thing, good and evil so bound together that it's impossible, sometimes, to separate them. You try so hard for control and order, and you get disorder. You put your faith in science, and you see ghosts. How do you know how to live your life? The ground is always shifting underneath your feet.

Out here in the heart of the country we've rationalized every inch of earth—all the straight lines of highway and farm and township—but mystery and wildness still lie waiting deep inside every particle of the world,

waiting to whirl or crack or ooze into our ordered lives, whether or not we've prepared for
it. And the more we deny it, cover it with concrete and lights, the tighter it crouches until it's
as small and ordinary as a tube of toothpaste
or as large as a crack in the foundations of the
world, and we have to pay attention.

I leave New Harmony late in the afternoon, heading for the half-moon of my own
confused township. The Harmonists still sleep.
Another day almost gone, and still, they're
waiting.

Halfway between New Harmony and Indianapolis, I pass two men butchering a deer.
The deer hangs by its legs from a tree, its front
hooves touching the earth. The men have hol-
lowed the deer body, the ribs turned inward,
something so graceful and terrifying in the
curve of the animal and the curve of the branch
it's hanging from, the men with their silver
knives and orange caps, their jump suits the
bronzy cinnamon of the oak leaves, the dark
flesh of the skinned deer mottled with fat,
white like the bark of the sycamores in the
woods behind them.

patterns

I live in the suburbs of Indianapolis, a city where we believe in the power of circles to keep you rooted in one place. You drive on any street and eventually you'll hit a circle which will bring you back to the place you began. Drive in toward the middle, and there's a circle there as well.

Good daughter that I am, I've lived here all my life, as has my family back for generations. My family has lived here almost without scandal, everyone fitting into patterned lives.

In the summer I swim in the same pool I swam in as a child. I sit in the chairs the mothers sat in. My children go to the same grade school that I did, and when it's time for the yearly carnival I stand behind the booths I used to stand in front of.

Sometimes I'll be driving my children through the quarter-moon of my township, and I'll see my five-year-old self and my ten- and fifteen- and twenty-year-old selves being driven past me, and I can almost see the knotted threads of my life, of all my neighbors' lives, as though what we are finally is the woven pattern of movement, a cat's cradle lifted, at the end, from the earth's fingers. And the cloth my family has woven is dense and thick, over and over the threads in the same place, dense but predictable with the same muted colors, the same streets. Other families have members who sail out like a hook on a fishing line, who take in all they can, the cloth loose and quirky but multicolored. Not us. We plodded, over and over, the same neighborhood, the same roads, a family of doctors and farmers and carpenters and occasional coal miners and maiden teacher aunts, until it was the city that did the changing. And while I guess, writing this, that we should feel somehow responsible for how the city's changed, since we've been here so long, I don't feel it. I don't know what that means. Except that we work our own corner, make our own cloth, the larger patterns not discernible, out of our control.

I'm addicted to stories of lives the way they seem in some autobiographies—seen backward, the wholeness the life has then, all hardened like a jewel. I wonder if the life felt that patterned while it was being lived. I doubt it. I like the ones where the characters seem to feel good in their bones from the beginning of their lives, no matter what happens around them—Maya Angelou, May Sarton—where the pain is there but the spirit is a leakproof boat that rides the waves. They're usually people who don't mind being alone. Sarton in her New England house with windows and light and flowers on the tables, Len Hubbard and his wife in their shantyboat on the Ohio River—their lives boiled down to purity, the clean light-filled interior of that boat with the closet built especially for the cello and a special place for the drawing pencils so that he always knows where to find them. My own house is so chaotic, all the books leaning haphazardly on the shelves and no shoe or sock lying with its mate. The Hubbards had rows of glass jars of river fish and vegetables that they grew along the banks in the summer. I love the icy stillness of their winter lives—selling his drawings when they needed the occasional dollar, the crystal nighttime sounds of their cello and the violin. The pattern of those lives. The economy. Maybe their lives were tortured and neurotic, but all I remember years after reading those

books is the clear light-filled spaces they created, the pure bubble of a life floating on the
darkness.

I want a life that feels like that. And what
I'm afraid of is that I have it and can't see it—
that it's in the pattern and the pattern will
never be visible to me. Or worse, that I have it
and see it and want sometimes for it to break
into its glittering pieces, to shatter into dusty
glass.

If the earthquake does come to Indiana,
there are places the ground will liquefy. Evansville, for instance, is built on ten miles of sand.
That part of Indiana is pocket country, cradled
by the Wabash and the Ohio. Sometimes I
think I'd like to live there. Where the roads
twist like ribbon candy and vapor trails from
jets curve south and north as they approach.
As though there's a magnetic field that turns
them away. There's no easy way to get there. I
want to be tucked away in the forgotten
pocket of Indiana, old lint in among the keys
and torn-off buttons and loose change of last
winter's coat, to ride in the sweet darkness of
that pocket until the ground is shaken so hard
the pocket melts and all of us—the Harmonists
and the woman at the loom and Tillich and the
elf woman and the woman in her husband's
thermal coat—no longer need to push away
the darkness with the four light walls of
homes. We will shake our patterns and melt

comfortably into the river the earth will become, into the dark, star-filled universe.

the tent

the guests

Under the tent it was humid and most of the guests had mud on their good shoes, and there were those black gnats that swarm in warm weather and now and then one flew in a guest's blinking eye. On the far side of the lawn, up a slight rise, more guests huddled under black umbrellas waiting for the young ushers who ran back and forth with no covering, gleeful as children in the gray rain, their rented suits soaked through.

But once the great aunts in their flowered dresses had been navigated across the slick mud under the pines and were seated, and even the grandmothers had made it safely inside, and all the guests had smoothed their hair and settled in, and it became clear that the tent would not leak and that it in fact cast its own sort of cheerful pearly light, the guests, not anxious as we ordinarily would be to leave the wedding and get onto other things, felt, every one of us, an unusual sense of peace. As though we had come, finally, to a place we could rest.

It's the tent, we said. And talk came easily. Coming from the isolation of our homes and the washed-out colors of a week of summer rain, we felt like one body.

It was hoped that the bride wouldn't be disappointed. Of course she had pictured this outdoor wedding in Disney animation—a brittle bright sun, the guests gathering like tame deer. But then she appeared underneath the pines accompanied by her father, laughing as he tilted a yellow umbrella above her head, drawing her grandmother's lace dress away from the mud, striding in the antique dress where the guests' footsteps had been tentative, her hair done up in flowers. It was clear she was not a fearful bride.

Inside the tent, the bride left her father and stood with the groom at the back to watch the musicians, both the bride and groom with the smiles and easy laugh of those used to being loved and admired, like a royal couple at some public exhibition. But never the least bit stuck up, their friends said, so alive, you can't help but love them.

Brothers and sisters from both families played and sang their own compositions, read poems they had written. Talent burned in the blood of both these families, flowing like lava from the parents, you could tell just by looking at them. We were sure the marriage of this boy and this girl would be the joining of two white-hot wires.

We stayed still as one by one the members of the wedding party broke from the group at the back of the tent and sailed forward. It was like the division of a clear cell seen under a microscope—that same brief clinging before the clean break and the self-containment. At the end the bride and groom walked toward their friends, almost throbbing with the joy, we said later, you couldn't take your eyes off them. Outside the tent, the rain fell harder, the trees smudged gray.

The bride's arms were bare, the neckline of the dress cut low, the groom's shirt was transparent from the rain. The bridesmaids' pink dresses blew about their ankles like fine hair.

There were poems by Rilke and Auden. The groom recited a poem he had written for his bride. His back was straight, his brown hair curling along the forehead and at the neck. The bride recited a poem she had written for him. Her voice broke as she praised his boyishness and the blaze of his step. The guests sat, witnesses, on cool metal folding chairs, white programs fanning the warm air.

The bride's mother read an essay she had written about her daughter. She was a beautiful woman, successful in real estate. She was the daughter thrown forward in time, firmly anchored, a secure rope thrown back for her daughter to navigate toward her. The groom's handsome father, a clergyman, performed the ceremony. Both sets of parents seemed well married. Though the bride's natural father was no longer married to the bride's mother, he read a short piece he had cut from a magazine and stood near the second husband, the yellow umbrella still dripping in his hand. The bride and her mother moved easily between them.

The guests whispered until we'd woven one story. It was understandable. The wife had simply kept growing while the first husband had settled in too easily. The second husband had the same lively eyes as the mother and the bride. And that was the key, we thought, to everything. In our best clothes, under the tent and the drumming rain that drew us together in the way all the makeshift card-table tents and caves of our childhood had done, we were drawn into the world of these children and of their parents and the continued possibilities of growth. People who had been homebound for years, afraid because of age or jobs or young children to take any but the smallest trips to adjoining states, thought of long vacations in China.

A little girl dressed in white appeared from among the guests and rang a bell. A boy lay a pink rose on a white table. The wedding party turned to the guests and sang Bob Dylan's "Forever Young."

After the ceremony there were assorted cheeses and pink champagne, a bowl of iced shrimp the size of a satellite dish, and a chef who carved rare steak. A band played soft rock. Did you hear? the guests whispered. They're spending the summer in the bride's grandparents' cottage near Brown County. They say they'll read and write poetry, take long bike rides before breakfast, drink wine outside in the late afternoon.

The ushers and the brothers of the bride and groom changed into Hawaiian shirts and khaki shorts or jeans. They stayed outside in the rain. Now and then one would run into the tent to get something to eat and to smile with joy and condescension at an aging relative who would grab his arm and ask about his life. Soon after, he would run from the tent, a shrimp in each hand, a can of beer hidden by one of the pine trees.

After dinner, some of the guests began to leave, the oldest first. We all felt years younger leaving the tent than when we'd entered. We got in our separate cars, adjusted the mirrors.

And then the change. There'd been too much to drink. We felt our faces melt like candle wax. There was an aching in the teeth.

Home, let's go home. We felt the years collapsing inward. We hadn't done half of what we'd planned.

t h e   f a t h e r

The barn was back away from the house and the party. He could hear raccoons or possums rummaging around the horse's feed. It was odd, this part of the city, these old disheveled brick at-one-time-estates with land along the river, stuck in the middle of a lower middle-class limestone ranch suburb. It was close to downtown but it felt rural, that kind of rural that had been controlled and then neglected, overgrown and wild, but not naturally so, borders of real woods with scrub in between. He hadn't wanted his wife to bring his children here. In the city the safest places were the most dense with buildings and any place like this — woods, parks, paths along the canal — felt dangerous whether they were or not. The people in the close-together houses could leave their doors unlocked. This single house had an alarm on every window.

His children grew up here without him.

He can watch us leaving. He knows what we'll talk about on the way home. A beautiful wedding, we'll say. But they're so young. They'll find out what it's really like. Of course let's pray it turns out magical for them. And of course, underneath, I'm ashamed to say our prayers are nothing like that at all. It's that shame that's driving me to think about this, what the father must feel — his daughter rising lighter than air, each car a wish, pulling her down.

He watches his wife leave, and her husband. Their arms around each other, his wife giggling like a girl. He used to hate them I'm sure, but that was before the deep married feeling had gone. He'd let it go and then was surprised when it washed back in a softer version. He felt affection for her now like he would for a sister if he'd had one. There would always be this tie between them. But she was too happy. It scared him. It was his belief that you can't lead a charmed life and expect your children to lead one too. It makes them weak, unsuspecting. Each family's tragedy lies hidden in the flesh and you've passed it on, their deaths a heaviness you carry with you. He'd told his wife to pull back, to turn down the flame. Most happy adults had unhappy childhoods. His wife said he was crazy and married that smiling man.

Nothing tragic could happen to him now except through his children, that was the only real suffering. He sat in the dark and watched.

His wife and her husband went into the house. Room by room, wherever she went, she drew a mark through the house with lights. And he remembered his daughter's soft fragile skin and the tracks her baton left in the air one summer night when she'd set it on fire.

the mother of the bride

I have this feeling, she told her husband, that something's out there in the dark. Hush, he said, it's your imagination, and she said, I know but I feel it out there and I'm afraid it doesn't mean well. They're leaving tonight, they've had too much champagne, it's a five-hour drive, someone uninvited has slipped in through the fence. Turn on the lights. Light the road like an airport runway.

She thought of Moses in the bullrushes, Oedipus in Corinth, of Jesus in Nazareth. She had tried to make herself a lightning rod to attract the gods. She had made herself happy.

She couldn't have been happy with him.

At first she thought it was the house. They'd lived in one of those fifties ranch houses built when no one seemed to care about light. The children filled the bedrooms. She was going to be an artist; it doesn't matter now what kind. It was music maybe, or painting. It doesn't matter. There wasn't much space. She didn't understand it, how she ended up in that house for one, although who ever understands, years later, how what seems like an inevitable decision was made. But she didn't understand why houses were ever built like that, what people could have been thinking. For decades they built those houses with small bedroom windows and the insides all catacombed with walls so there were windows on only one side of each room. You had to have electric lights on the brightest days or live with the dark. She didn't understand it, what it meant. Was everyone so depressed then because of the bomb that they wanted to wallow in it or were they so happy that it didn't matter? Maybe they wanted to hide, to burrow in. She couldn't remember. Whatever it was, she put all her energies into a furious obsessive mothering and into that house, into changing it to sell to someone else.

And they sold it, at a big profit. Before she knew it she was doing it with the next house and the next until she began looking at houses not as homes but as places to sell. The money came so easily. It wasn't until the fourth house that she realized that it was her husband who'd grown dark, and she found a new one whose spirit was a clear glass window.

the new husband

All right. He'd go down to check. But the fences were high, there were plenty of lights, the band was still playing. It was all a success, in spite of the rain. The rain was lucky, he said. It rains for good weddings and there are a lot of sunny funerals.

But he would go out if it would make her happy. He understood, her only daughter leaving, how she must feel.

It had stopped raining. There were still several cars parked up near the house. He walked toward the music. The caterer's tent was dark, but the wedding tent still glowed pink and gold. There were candles lit on the tables. The young people were dancing. All the boys had changed clothes and the girls stayed in their thin party dresses. His daughter, her lace dress, her hair pinned with flowers. She looked so like his wife. She was dancing with one of her new husband's friends. You didn't need to see her face to know that she was happy. One time, he heard her say to the boy, I counted, and I had seven yellow dresses. At the end of the song she spun, and her skirt bloomed out around her. She ran over to her husband and laid her head against his chest. Her eyes were dreamy, her shoulders bare. The lace glittered in the candlelight. She took a sip of her husband's champagne. He had loosened his shirt.

The groom seemed such a boy. He had a scholarship in the fall. We won't mind poverty, he'd said earlier in the evening, quite earnestly. We'll find a way to buy theater tickets and wine, he'd said. And two cats.

Neither one of them knew a damned thing about the world. He felt uneasy. He did wish them well, didn't he? He loved them, didn't he? It's just that this new son seemed such a boy.

The bride saw him standing outside the tent. She smiled at him, seemed happy to see him. It was his wife when he first met her. Come in!

He walked in through the candles. Her hair had smelled like flowers. She was married to that unhappy man. She hadn't danced in years when she danced with him. Her hair had smelled like flowers. When she had first found a way to be with him, and after, when she went back home, she said she was ashamed to touch the children. Now her daughter was running over and pulling on his sleeve as naturally as if he were her real father. Dance, she said, and he forgot why his wife had sent him out here, and with a look up at where she was probably watching through the window, he waved her down and began to dance.

the bride and
her husband

My parents seemed so unnecessary, so unimportant, when I was younger. I seldom thought of them. Were you like that? Isn't it funny how much alike we are?

Well, I thought they must not think about me much more than I thought about them and then one spring I took my babysitting money and I went out and bought a yellow dress and when I came back my mother told me I was having another yellow spring and she got out a photo album and we looked back years and we counted seven different yellow dresses and springs when I wore only yellow blouses and carried yellow umbrellas and baby springs with yellow hairbows and dolls with yellow hair. And she showed me lavender springs and bright red springs and no-color springs and it was clear that while I hadn't noticed her, she had weighed and sifted and named each one of my seasons, and it was an odd feeling, to be that noticed, or rather to be that loved and not notice it. Were you like that? Did you ever feel like that? Isn't it all so strange?

My mother was going to be a musician I think, but she gave it up, I don't know why. They're all so cautious. We will never ever do that, give anything up. My father is afraid of flying, it keeps him home. He never noticed me. My mother will fly, but she keeps her eyes on the ground constantly, as though it's her attention and not the pilot that keeps the plane in the air.

They would die if they knew all the things I've done. They have no idea. I remember, when I was a girl, my mother keeping her eye on me whenever I was near water. I could never swim in the pool without someone else by. She thought she kept me safe, and at night in summers I'd go out through a window and back by the river, you know there's that cliff, sometimes it was muddy and I'd slide down on my shoes, it was so dark back there I could only tell by the sound on cloudy nights when I was getting close to the water, and I'd have to grab on to a bush to stop. I'd walk along the river by myself and sometimes I'd see a man pulling a silver fish out of the water or just sitting or throwing in stones, and there were rusted cans and broken bottles, and sometimes in the morning I'd hear about a skull someone dug up along the river, but I kept going back. At first there were witches down there and pirates and later boys and one spring a whole bank full of violets and I remember standing surrounded by them and seeing myself like a girl in a book or a painting. Nothing could really touch me.

And weren't they funny tonight? My father with that umbrella even under the tent. He looked ready to open it again like he didn't trust that it wouldn't rain in here, the way they were all so serious and nervous before the wedding, I think they love us really, and they've all gone now, asleep, except for my stepfather over there drinking in the corner, he seems older tonight than I've noticed before.

But what I want to say is that we're special and I always want us to have this wildness, to never hole up, become safe. Let's always live on houseboats, in tents under the stars. Let's never buy a thing we have to keep a lock on or that we have to build a house around or that we can't move. I want it to always feel like that night we took those back roads down a gravel path to that old rickety fire tower, do you remember? Hundreds of feet high with a sign that said not to climb and we both laughed and climbed to the top where we could feel it sway and we could see nothing but woods and no people for miles and you said that if we fell it would be months until we were found and still we stayed up there, giddy, everything, the tower and the treetops and the hills a movement and a dance, and we were part of it, like we could fly.

Earlier I saw one of the flower girls crying that gasping, choking crying over something, her mother holding her, rocking her, and I felt myself feeling like the one doing the rocking and at the same time like the one being rocked. Someday we'll be our parents and our children will be us and I wonder what we'll feel and what they'll feel and if they'll know that when we were them we wondered what it would be like. I feel light, like I've been drinking ether, like the tent is whirling and my skirt is the tent and this has all been happening for a long, long time. Do you feel like that? Isn't it funny how much alike we are?

seeds: a meditation on the body

It is the light at the center of every cell.

—Mary Oliver

There are seeds on the deck where it juts awkwardly from the plane of the house. Dry brown husks on the cracked boards, seeds spilled like grain down the slope of the umbrella. White seeds spin past my face and land in my daughter's hair. They collect along the fence like lint in a child's pocket.

Sometimes, in the spring and fall, the air's so thick with seeds it's hard to breathe. Sometimes that vision of the earth as one whirl of erotic, glittering matter seems much less strange to me.

I think of those television documentaries, Disney films where seeds crack, time-lapse, rapid motion. A black seed in the beak of a bird, a seed with thorns resting in a fox's coat as though the fox, the bird, existed only as a means, for that seed, of locomotion. The bird can try to deny its hunger. The fox can say how dare a seed develop burrs just to hitch a ride with me; keep your evolution to yourself, you stupid lethargic seed, stay separate. I can't be counted on, generation after generation, to walk right by you just when you're looking for the next bus out of town. But the seed, all blank and unresponsive as a stone, rides the fox or bird right out of that thicket of questions. It never even tries to answer. The questions are all answered, for the seed, in the ride and the cracking teeth or in the lack of them. And in the slow unfolding of the stem and root and leaf.

In another of those Disney documentaries, there's a kind of seed that has an L-shaped tail, and when it falls to the ground, in the sped-up time of the camera, it looks as though it throws the tail from one side to the other in the slightest wind. The seed crawls away from the mother plant with all the will its vegetable soul can muster. Wise seed. Benevolent universe.

In the next frame they show seeds sucking

the life from 100-year-old trees, and a seed
which grows into a sort of green pot with a lid.
A pitcher plant, I think they call it. It has no
chloroplasts or something. All it can eat is pre-
digested rot. So it lives in swamps and turns itself into a cauldron full of rotting matter, a
soup which attracts flies and bees and other insects. They drown and bubble. I watch the
plant as it lures the bees, but I wish I hadn't
seen it. I would prefer to go for years and years
without remembering that particular vision of
the universe: that God is in the gazelle as it
falls and in the lion who eats her. That every
living thing is both the hunter and the hunted,
the eater and the eaten in this cosmic soup, this
hungry mouth, this constant exchange of energy.

Women newly stricken with baby madness, wheeling the clear plastic cribs down the
hospital corridors at night, the amber lighting
low against the ground like an airport runway.

Twice now I've curdled blood into milk
and held the cup out to the sleeping ones, saying Drink this. Drink this down.

My children were both c-sections. Where
did I come from? they ask. This is the line, I
say, where the surgeon reached into the darkness and pulled you out. I saw you shut your
eyes. I saw you open them. The doctor pro-

duced you with a flourish, a magician with his flowers, a waiter with a flaming dessert.

When I held my first child, I knew that some day I would die. And sometimes at night now when the children cry in their sleep, I know in a way they don't that some day they will die as well. And I feel, oddly, like I owe them an apology. Like I dragged them, against their wills, into consciousness. Not dragged exactly. It was a snap. Like that sharp snap of the wrist as you open a paper bag.

I was awake for the surgery. My head was draped off from the rest of my body so I couldn't watch.

But there was a dome mirror, and the tilt was right, and I watched it all. First a line of blood appearing on the stomach and then the skin pulled back. In Indiana, during deer season, you'll see cars with skinned animals riding on the hood, or deer run over on the highway—the way they deflate so quickly into slippery ooze. What filled the dome was as gory as that, as bloody as a slaughterhouse. I was numb from the neck down, nothing but a thinking head. I wondered how much more of myself I could lose and still be me. I wondered about the soul. I wondered about the resurrection of the body. You think too much, my husband says to me. He means it kindly.

I remember I was freezing cold, that I had

put makeup on that morning, and curled my hair, I have no idea why. It was like I needed to preserve the mask, like a Japanese warrior preparing for ritual suicide. When I felt that jangling insect sound that comes prior to the loss of consciousness, I was terrified, felt that I had been nine-tenths erased and was about to lose the most important tenth, that my spirit was cradled in the mask like the baby in its cushion of blood or like water in a bowl.

It's still easier to explain the surgeon's scalpel to my children—they picture it clean and simple as a letter opener on an envelope— than it is to explain sex. Save that for later, when they're old enough to understand. By the way, I'll say, there's a little more to it than I told you. I forgot to mention this hungry engine at the heart of things. For a while it will become your Great Unified Theory, your religion. Someday you might make and maintain or not a marriage in response to or defiance of the siren call of seeds.

For seven years I lived in New Castle, Indiana—a town famous for roses. Some German woman in the 1800s ran a greenhouse, and she hybridized a rose that had blossoms as big as a man's fist and stems that could reach, if you carried one, from your waist to the ground. There are pictures in the county museum, in among Victorian hair wreaths and paintings of the county fathers and mothers and famous local disasters (the day the Goodyear blimp got tangled in the power lines in Metamora), of ballrooms in New York decorated with those monster roses. They're in the Historical Society Museum in Henry County, Indiana. You can go there and see if this is real or fabrication.

The woman died and no one else could hybridize those roses. You couldn't grow them from the seed. The seed grew into scrawny, nothing little things. Or maybe they had no seed, were sort of gelding eunuch roses. I can't remember.

Years before I even thought of having children I went to a doctor who was known for her stitches. She was a doctor and a quilter, and women went to her with their pregnancies. Her stitches are amazing, a nurse said to me, and I'll always remember it because, for some reason, it made me uncomfortable in some innocence I had then. She'll sew you up, the nurse said, tighter than a virgin.

It was the same discomfort I remember when a pregnant woman I worked with in high school had her water break back in the coffee room, her Hooks Drugstore smock soaked with warm amniotic fluid, the same discomfort I felt a few years later, still before children, when a nursing woman in still another break room had her milk let down, and a wet circle the size of a half-dollar grew on her blouse over a nipple and all the matrons laughed and remembered how their bras had turned this crusty yellow and how and where their milk had embarrassed them and whether their husbands had liked the taste.

It was the animal part of me that, before children, I had trouble with, and perhaps still have some trouble with, am afraid at times of drowning in. I only know that after giving myself over to the seed for all those months of pregnancy, the animal feels less and less like something I live in opposition to and more like the thing I live inside, or rather, the thing I am. It's when the body goes one way and the will another that I split apart.

I've lived in denial of the body and I've lived in denial of the soul. And I've lived, for brief periods, in faith. In both places I've felt blinded.

The place I live best is in the small green open space between them.

You think too much, my husband says to me. He's a practical man, and good with flowers.

The frustrating thing about thinking too

much, he says, is that it only leaves you right where you began, with your own voice asking questions. I decided a long time ago that there are questions I'll never know the answer to.

So what do you think about? I ask him.

Things I can know the answer to, he says. Like who will win the Bears game. Sunday night I tune in and there it is, the score.

I tell him about this new book that proves irrefutably that consciousness is made up of little things like computer chips, each one of which registers something like a color or the direction of a line or motion. All the chips work together to tell you that you're seeing a car or a tulip; there's nothing central like a soul to tie it all together. The book explains that the greatest mysteries are chemical and really very simple. Just computer chips and firing neurons. In the illustrations, they make the neurotransmitters look like those little squarish horseshoe-shaped things that attach wires to batteries.

We're out behind the house. I'm talking. He's mulching roses and cutting off the flowers before they go to seed. All the plants want are seeds. All we want are blossoms.

This guy believes that when we look at something, there's this incredible amount of activity going on up there in the brain, like a wild shuffling of cards, and we go through all the possibilities before letting the correct one win. The other possibilities are like drafts, but you're not in the least aware of them.

Do you believe that? he asks me. No, I say, not a bit, but it's interesting to think about. It sort of de-mystifies things, says you are who you are and you should just relax and interface or not.

And if it were true, I say, it would explain so much. For instance, that writers are people who simply keep discarded drafts; my brain is a museum of old paper, old photo albums. I can't just look at that rose and be done with it.

He puts a white cone over one of the rose bushes. Sometimes you can see it working, I say. Like if you look out the window this winter and for one second forget you put that cone there. You might think that there's a white dog or a child in a white coat or an angel crouching up near the house. Silly me, you'll say, and then forget it. If that happened to me, I say, I never would.

"The longer the radius of vision," Wendell Berry says, "the wider the circumference of mystery." Mystery doesn't feel empty to me; it feels, in fact, like the thing that drives the emptiness away. In order to see the edge of it, I have to travel again and again through a cloud of words, in a kind of attention that's as close as I can get to prayer. I envy people who get there more easily than that.

I remember some mystic's insistence that God is the resonance that vibrates between beings, the song at the center of the seed, something very much like love. My husband plants roses, and I hear the song straining through the white noise of the existential hum.

We're on our way to the State Fair, a friend and I and our four children.

I've been to the fair every year of my life. My children have been there every year of theirs. Every year we see the giant pumpkin and the giant zucchini, the stalks of corn, the lamb chops grilling in a tent outside the barn of well-combed 4-H baby lambs, the beef steaks grilling outside the cattle barn. (There is, or used to be, a carcass contest at the fair— teenagers standing in front of the iced and skinned meat of their recent pet cow, praying for satin ribbons.)

We park out by the horse barns. We'll start with horses, then pigs, then sheep then cows then chickens. End with midway, corn dogs, and tractors.

The light is filtered through green variegated windows in the first barn, there's a blue harness hanging by a stall, country music on the radio, a black-and-white television sitting on top of a refrigerator. It's a hot day, and hazy humid. The air is slick with pollen.

There are human footprints in the mud on the barn floor, but no horses; harness racing was last weekend, and the horses have gone home.

The kids aren't disappointed. They're fascinated by the grainy image on the black-and-white TV. Four kids and two adults, we stand quietly staring at the soundless screen, the electronic communal hearth. We can look and see the storyteller's image burning in the flames, not floating in our separate heads around them.

We tell the kids to come on, and we head out of the barn. Beyond the empty horse barns, before the first strip of corn dogs and lemon shake-up trailers, there's an exhibit of army vehicles. Half of them are painted with green camouflage, the other half painted desert brown.

The boys run up to a tank and start climbing on it. A man in a desert-tinted uniform stands by the tank and smiles at them.

During the recent war, the neighborhood children talked about it as though it were a football game. Who's winning, they'd ask, the Iraqi team or the U.S. team?

My son collects football cards, and there's one in the 1991 set of U.S. soldiers in those gas masks that make them look like enormous insects. The soldiers are gathered around a television in the desert, watching the Super Bowl. Shortly after the war ended, Topps brought out packs of Desert Storm cards in the same rapid way they put together collecting cards for hit movies.

You know, my friend says, this is a horrible thing to say, but in a way I miss the war.

It's like the summer we had the Pan Am Games, she says. I've never been much interested in sports, but I really missed them when they left. The malls were filled with people speaking Spanish and Portuguese. There were all the flags and banners.

The war was just like that, she says. I forgot the bills, I forgot that it was yucky winter weather, I didn't mind when the kids got the flu and we had to spend hours in front of the television. Sam had been all depressed, saying he hated his life, threatening to leave us, and the war somehow pulled us back together, gave us something outside ourselves to talk about, something we agreed on.

She goes up to the soldier by the tank. How is it being back? she asks him and he says it's been easy. She tells him we all appreciate what they've done for us. He says it felt good to come home to all those yellow ribbons.

I'm looking at the paint job, trying to see if there's any green underneath the brown, any sign of haste. There isn't. The army had desert-painted equipment way before the war, the soldier says. I wonder whose job it is to predict the color of camouflage you'll need next and what a strange job that would be, and I remember that both church and secular law make a distinction between crimes carried out in the heat of passion and those carried out with conscious malice.

They're dirty people, the soldier is saying to my friend. They'd piss in the desert and then put down a prayer rug and start praying.

A man in his thirties, pink T-shirt and jet-black sunglasses, comes over to ask the soldier questions. He points to a helicopter. That's not the baddest piece of equipment, the soldier says. The Apache is the baddest. It has night-time capability. That thing comes in, and you don't know what the hell happened to you.

He's got a joystick over there that he flies like an Atari. There's the slew on the front, that lens like a giant eye. He's got 40mm grenade launchers, a 7.62 machine gun good for 4,000 rounds.

They fly in low, over the trees, underneath the radar.

The soldier talks about the smoke from all the oil fires, how at the end of his stay the day-time started looking like the night. He's been home a couple of months, he says, but the army's getting ready to send him down someplace in South America. Guess we'll shoot us some monkeys, he says.

As far as I'm concerned, the pink T-shirt man is saying to my friend, Schwarzenegger gets no credit for this. It was some little geeky guy in a computer room someplace who blew up all those Iraqis. Iranians? Iraqis? Which one was it.

Iraqis, my friend says. And it's interesting you called him Schwarzenegger instead of Schwartzkopf. You substituted the Terminator.

When women are out together with their children, there are these sudden moments of panic when one of the women loses track of where the children are. Sometimes the moments of panic come even when you're out without the children in a crowd. You get so used to having them with you, and the fear that something terrible will happen to them runs so deep.

Where's Laura? I ask, realizing I haven't seen her for a couple of minutes. Over there, my friend points to the Apache. Up there, with Brooke.

The boys are still listening to the soldier, fascinated by the tank. I'll go over with the girls, I tell my friend.

There are no soldiers by the helicopter and the girls are both sitting in the cockpit. They're punching buttons and playing with the joystick, but nothing happens. The girls look at me with hunger — put in a quarter, mommy, my daughter says, we want it to go up and down.

This is real, I tell them, a real helicopter. And I relax, grateful that both of the little girls are together in one place, and having fun, and safe so that for a minute or two I can think my own thoughts and not worry about their safety.

The girls see what they think is a cowboy, and they climb down out of the cockpit and go over and look at a man dressed in a green jumpsuit and green hat. My daughter and her friend like your uniform, I tell him. What kind is it? I'm in a cavalry unit, he says, like in the movies, he tells the girls.

There's still cavalry? I ask. We perform the same function, he says, only with helicopters instead of horses.

The horses are all gone, my daughter says.

The cavalry scout moves over by the Apache. The man in the pink T-shirt comes over to ask him questions. The boys come with him, and they start to climb up into the cockpit.

No son, the scout says, putting his arm on Steven's shoulder. There are explosives in this thing.

There was a sign on the side of the helicopter: This aircraft contains a cartridge escape system equipped with explosive charge. Like James Bond, the scout says.

I crouch down and hold my daughter's body close. There's a tent, my son is telling me, where a woman will paint our faces with desert or jungle camouflage.

Let's go, I say to my friend. I want to see the giant vegetables, the world's sweetest pie, the sleepy-eyed children drinking Big Red and lounging on lawn chairs in the cattle barn. I want to see where they change these things into tractors and plowshares. I want to be amazed by the microscopic stitches on row after row of quilts hanging in the domestic arts building by the cross-stitched God Bless Our Home.

The hardest thing for a human being to do is to see another human being as real. The easiest way to justify killing is to separate the individual body from the individual soul. If another human being is only animal, in the way we de-soul the animal, it doesn't matter if we kill him. If another human being is only spirit then, still, it doesn't matter.

After the fair, we drop off my friend and her two children. My son is sitting on the seat behind me. Mom, he says, this is a dumb question, but can you tell me if I died, I mean can you tell me if I'm dead and this is a dream I'm having.

I reach back to where he's sitting, and I pat his knee. Feel this? You didn't die, I'm right here with you, and it's real.

My daughter's in the seat beside me. She bends her knee and watches her foot rise. How did they make that, she asks. Your brain told your foot to go up in the air, I say. Why do I move? she asks. Because you're alive, I tell her. How do they make glass, she asks? It's made from sand, I say.

My son and four of his friends climb onto the roof of the mini-barn. Five boys on an eight-foot rectangle, fifteen feet off the ground. Get down, I yell through a shut window.

They can't hear me, so I run outside. Laura and her friends follow me. Chrome bicycles, discarded shells, lie in a pile against the barn, all twisted and sharp and glinting.

The dog jumps up on one of my daughter's friends, and the little girls start screaming. They leap on top of a table which is on top of the deck which is, because the ground slopes, eight feet off the ground.

The wind is blowing like crazy, the leaves of the cottonwoods are shaking their heads at me. Bad mother. Bad mother. You there, with a yard full of precariously balanced children.

Get down! I yell at all of them, and I grab

the dog by the collar. All of you, right now, get back on the ground.

Why don't you have a scavenger hunt, two teams, and you go out and hunt for seeds.

Steven and his best friend Zachary and Laura and her best friend Katie are on one team, the other two boys and one girl on another.

I have this pastoral vision of children filling a grocery bag with dried catalpa beans and maple seeds.

Instead, fifteen minutes later, Steven and Laura's team comes into the kitchen, all four of them with their arms full of gourds and green tomatoes and apples and dark green cantaloupes that had fallen off the stems and never ripened.

Before I have time to really think about this, the boys have knives in their hands, the girls spoons because they're only four and they know I wouldn't let them use the knives, and they're doing a sort of *Psycho* shower scene in the kitchen with these vegetables. Steven and Zach jab the knives into the gourds, pound them against the table, squash them with their shoes until the seeds begin to ooze through cracks. Laura and Katie take the softer bodies, the tomatoes and peppers, the things they can mutilate with the straight end of a spoon.

For a minute, for two minutes, I'm reminding myself how I want to be one of those mothers who lets her kids make potions of dish soap and food coloring and put them in the freezer, to make volcanoes on the kitchen floor with vinegar and baking soda, to make salt maps and papier-mâché, one of those mothers with atlases open on the sofa and globes spinning across the floor, that romantic mother vision.

So I try to ignore the vegetable slime dripping down the cabinets, the cantaloupe guts on the table, the seeds sticking to the windows and the children's hair.

But five minutes later I'm sending them back outside, this shrieky voice coming from my mouth. Not in the house, I'm saying. Not here inside the house.

I give them newspapers covered with slime and seed and a coffee can to drop the seeds down into once they're separate from the goo.

And I start cleaning. I sponge off the table, the cabinets. I clean the windows with paper towels and vinegar, the floor with ammonia. Seeds stick to the sponge, to my hand, and when I'm done I rinse them, watch the seeds spill down the drain. I work like fury for ten minutes. Old husks. Old husks. There are seeds inside of us that want to explode. In ten minutes the kitchen is clean of all traces of the slaughter.

the garden city church of christ

Sunday morning in Garden City. The Church of Christ opens wide its doors. There's a wire fence holding back the fields. A playground for the children. An entire row of parking, near the door, for the elderly. Every morning she circles twelve times around the outside of the fence.

The parking lot fills with cars, the early risers, old people who for years and years have

walked inside the doors as easily as someone
laying down a magazine to answer the phone
or, gentler still, a mother laying counted cross-
stitch on a chair and turning to a child—a simple, gentle act. It could never be like that for
her.

Good morning, sister, the old people say
to her and they open the glass doors to the
church and the reflected green of weeds and
her reflected dress bend and slide right off the
door, replaced by pavement. The old people
open up the folding chairs and join the others
around a potted plant where they nod and talk
until the young ones come racing past them.

Please understand. The woman walking
loves the Garden City Church of Christ: wheel-
chairs in the aisle, the folding screen that's always pushed back for the overflow. The teen-
age girls in their short dresses with their
braided summer hair, the boys in freshly laun-
dered jeans, the old men and women with the
bony hands, the beautiful-eyed old woman
who plays the organ, the plump mothers with
their shy, serious husbands, the crying, spit-
uppey babies passed from hand to hand, the
haughty, off-key choir with on high-angelic
smiles, the preacher with his dark hair and the
sound system with the taped orchestra and the
taped 1,000 voices that rise up perfectly beneath the wavering amplified country voice of

the soloist. In spite of everything, she loves it all.

At the Garden City Church of Christ they notice if you don't attend; if you're ill or shut-in, the elders come to your house on Sunday afternoon with a little black box, velvet-lined like a flute box, filled with already blessed holy communion.

Sometimes she thinks that she's the only person in the world who wants inside and can't go in. All she can do is take another step, step after step in this circle. Twelve perfect circles, one on top of the other. The first one made the way for all the rest and she prays that she's a planet so fixed in orbit now that she won't plunge in toward the warm fiery windows in the winter or fly off into the chaff, lost, in the spring.

She has to keep moving. It's the moving that matters, that keeps her where she is.

She's been inside.

Two years ago, an entire spring. Every day the sun shook out the world like a crisp, bleached sheet on the line, wafer-thin, and it melted on her tongue.

The story grew in her head like any story. What amazes her now is how slowly and logically it grew, how it seemed as normal to think it as it is to think those things that everyone agrees on. It was seamless, the way the gray world streamed into this Technicolor one. Not the sudden jolt of the Wizard of Oz—it was all one piece, and so she didn't question it.

I won't bore you with the story. It was any crazy Western woman's story. A bride-of-Christ story. She tried to buy two cars and a condominium. She bought fifteen purses, religious magnets for the refrigerator, sack loads of leftover Easter candy. God told her to do it, she thought that. The fields turned to straw and she saw cellophane, it was there to unwrap, to buy, it was hers to take.

Then ten weeks in the hospital. Drugs that make her hand shake. They give them to you in a nut cup like a party.

When she went in she could talk like a bolt of lightning. She didn't need a lick of sleep. She was happy. Then one day after she'd been there nearly ten weeks the O.T. came through with a parrot on her arm and she could control her laughter. She was cured, the doctor said, and he sent her home.

Afterward, the world outside the hospital was too immense, her bed the only safety. She felt like if she touched herself she'd rub off slick dust like talcum.

She could lie in bed and see her body spinning fast like one of those sped-up time things in a movie, all the ages flying by like you'd peel an egg and her shrinking into an old woman and the flesh rotting off the bone, the bone shrinking to powder, the wind scattering her all to Kingdom Come. She flew apart and couldn't find the way to pull herself together. She wanted to see the reel rewind, to see her body rushing in a whirling roar like flakes of iron back to this magnet which was her or not her, she doesn't know, whatever it is, the center of her, the gravity and core.

That's what she lost. That's what she couldn't find.

When she got home she went to bed and didn't get up for two months. Her mother fed her liquids with a spoon. She called the doctor; he said it was normal after how high she'd been.

That's when he ordered her to walk, and her father got her out of bed. Move, he said. Walk.

Why? she asked. He said because she had no choice.

The squares of windows and the door were an unnatural metallic bright. She couldn't move toward them on her own, but every day her father got her up and every day she slithered closer to the door and one day when the clouds were thick as blankets she made it outside and she stood on the front porch and decided that maybe she could stand the daylight in small doses, covered over.

Two miles a day, the doctor said, to get you on an even keel. Maybe that will save you.

This is hilly land, it heaves and pitches. She couldn't imagine two miles, couldn't see two flat miles. She thought and thought. The Garden City Church of Christ, she said to her mother and father, and they looked at her suspiciously. Why there? they asked, she said because it's easy ground. Her father measured the outside of the fence. Twelve times around, he said, would make two miles.

So she walks around the edge of the Garden City Church of Christ. She can't go in. The windows dark and liquid, glazed with trees and cars and Sunday clothes. She's nothing but these legs and the will to take each step. Religion and love are the same to her as craziness; it's all the same kind of drowning.

Her parents work six days a week at Cummins Engines. She lives with them. She loves them. There's no other place for her.

They have a small orchard. In mid-summer, they box the globes of cherries. They throb as red as a child's crayon.

Her parents are Methodists, lukewarm, they go to church if there's nothing else to do or if they think of it. That's the way it should be, they told her then; religion has its place like everything.

In the front of the hymnal there are instructions for singing. Don't let your voice rise

above the others. The minister's voice is rational. The cross is bare and smooth as a ball bat.

Everything is very everyday to them, ordinary. The world to them is like it once was for
her: filled with real trees, real strawberries, real
and solid homes and lawns that rock you like
your mother rocked you. They have no idea
that it all could disappear, like that, beneath
their feet.

They have foil pie plates tied to all the
cherry trees. They twist and flash in the sun.

She would give anything for the universe
to seem rock hard again.

A couple in a pickup truck drop their son
off at the door. He holds a soft Bible in both
hands. (The leather on her Bible curled in at
the edges like a shell. She would walk along
here opening the book at random for an answer; in pieces she read it, fragments. She remembers how it felt in her hands, the snapping
sound when it bent, like a pocketbook closing.
She'd open that book, focused on it like a
Ouija board, and for a while it spoke to her,
but finally the shell-like edges contracted and it
would fall open to a barren picture of the holy
desert or the impenetrable black of the binding, and whatever it was she once saw was
curled deep inside the shell, pulsing and raw as
a wound.)

Do you see? She has this fragile streak of

bluish blood between her eyes, thin as a broomstraw or a baby's vein. She was born with it. It's always been there.

Sometimes beauty is unbearable. That spring she was crazy, on sunlit Sunday afternoons at her uncle's A-frame it would almost hurt. She'd be out there with all her cousins, all the shadows home, the pines dripping, oozing so every needle glistened, and her uncles spread out around the pond with poles, fishing for the bass they'd planted there and throwing them back in. In the yard her aunts uncovered the dishes, set out the spoons, the charcoal gray and hot and ashen, the cars and trucks huddled around the clearing like cattle. It all came so easily: the ribs that split on the grill, the bread that rose under the hands of the women, the bubbles that rose in the cans of soda, the whole world lit and shouting at the sky.

Hush.
The Garden City Church of Christ is dark inside, the walls and floors and seats a shadowed green, the green of a leaf away from the sun, a long long carpet to walk down. And up in front a wall of black river stones, shiny as the center of a cut. And in the center of the wall that large aquarium of water, a square of

gray water with stairs hidden behind the wall, a white room hung with robes.

That spring she was immersed there. And after she made her walk and the preacher stopped the singing for her and put his arms around her and told the congregation her sad and common story, and they all sat there waiting while she went behind the wall and took off her flowered dress, and some of them cried for her because the preacher told the story well and some of them did not listen, impatient to get home to dinner or their own unweeded gardens, to geraniums that needed pinching and roses hanging fat against a fence, wishing she had waited for a Sunday when the preaching hadn't been so long, when the children's choir hadn't sung with their slow gathering and their long procession out. Though many in the congregation were with her as she put on the long white robe and walked up the dark steps and stood there waiting to walk with the preacher down the slick steps into the milky water and the swirl of chlorine.

Like the Scriptures say: the earth is an old robe, the earth reels and rocks like a drunken man. There's no place you can live, she thought, except in this clean water. And every moment new.

And she saw all their faces through the glass, looking up at her, and he held her waist and bent her head back down into the water and when she came back up the entire universe swirled like paint or one of those flat galaxies of stars you see in movies spiraling and forming, and she took it all in with new breath and she breathed out fire to the trees, all of the world's breathing a blessing, an exchange, and for that moment only she was breathing in the chorus of the body of Christ, participating consciously in the chorus of the body of Christ as easily as birds celebrate their own frail and buoyant bodies.

The young boy goes inside the Church of Christ. It will take a while for him to get adjusted to the dark. But the gray will pass. It's like the gray the grass turns from dried clippings. Rake them off and you're shocked by all the green. Even the windows in the sanctuary are a bubbled wavering green. The whole place feels like a pond.

If he's still, he'll see it like something rising, coming into focus from the bottom.

Hush. The prayer.

This is the quiet that terrifies her.

The boy will sit in a pew at the back, and throw in the line with its glinting hook. The walking girl is afraid he'll never get it back, that it will hook some fish too large for him and he'll be dragged down under, down to where he won't know how to swim. It was a line like that that pulled her in or didn't save her, and she's never found her way back up. Maybe he's choking now, he's near her, she can almost hear him—lungs filled up with water, mud, and slimy weeds.

She could never quite explain this, never get it exactly right, but she's afraid he'll sink so deep he can't speak, his soul gone or hiding back there some place deep between his eyes.

Every day she saw the earth explode and vanish. There wasn't a thing she could see worth rising for.

She needs to get to him, to tell him there's a whirlpool twisting near the center of everything, even here, in Garden City. A black hole, deep space, earthquake, tornado, it wants to suck you in. You skate on the edge like the lip of a glass or you float so far out that you can't feel the turning, but it's there, and it's pulling him, and eventually he'll feel it or he feels it now.

The air bends like water. The girl walks and holds her hand in front of her. She looks for his hand, the cup of his fingers.

She prays that he will make it through. That he will swim with every muscle, hard, through an underground cave full of ocean, that after the prayer and the preaching, after the announcements and the responsive reading, before the benediction, all that holy buoyant ritual, the place he will come out is a place filled with light. And that when he does he'll reach back up and take her with him.

Because she's drowning in the quiet, in the center of the pull. Where the sycamores are rooted but edgy as lightning. Where the church is a building and the fence holds back the fields. Where the earth rolls like a river. The earth heaves like a river. The earth rocks like a river. And she's a weak swimmer, with no place to stand.

the problem of evil

They watched this on the news, and they pieced it together. It was morning, last spring, already a summer heat.

It happened at a grain elevator up near the lakes.

This man pulled up in front of the office and parked beside his father's car. Someone was using an auger to load corn into a company truck. The auger was turning slowly, only a trickle of corn moving through it.

He went inside the office. It was all closed up, hot and stale.

His father wasn't behind the desk. He looked through the window back to where the others parked when they came in. The lot was empty. All he could hear was the auger and the click of corn.

Maybe it was the sharp sunlight, the man said later, the defined clean edges of trees and shadows—everything that morning so suddenly *there* for his father after the long winter. Whatever it had been, somehow the man knew.

Afterward the witnesses said the man had worked for two hours, attaching himself to a lifeline and digging in the corn. The grain sucked at his waist as he dug. He was joined by other men who heard his screaming.

Afterward an expert told how it could happen, how a man falling into an unloading bin becomes immobile in three seconds, waist-deep in grain in nine, buried in about eighteen, how it would take 2,000 pounds of force to remove him once he's three feet in.

During the interview, later, all the man could talk about was his father as this spirit hovering over his childhood, warning of dangers.

It was hard for him to accept, his father's lack of caution, his death without warning on a perfect spring day.

A woman sits on the couch, her legs covered by an unfinished afghan, the crochet hook still hanging in an open loop in the middle of a row. Now and then she makes another stitch. Inside, in the dark, she makes rows while outside, in the sun, her husband does the same. For miles and miles around there are men making rows, children in school in rows of chairs, graves and church pews and lines of days stretching.

In the evening her husband comes in for dinner. His face and arms are coated with dust. He smiles down at her, comments on the chill in the house, and heads for the shower. She smiles at him and gets up to fix dinner. She knows she looks fairly industrious—the house straight because neither one of them does much to ever mess it up, her crocheting. It doesn't matter to him what she does with her days as long as she seems happy. It could take her twenty years to finish the afghan and he would assume that twenty years is how long it should take her.

She moves around the kitchen inefficiently —two or three times to the same cabinet for spices that are right next to each other. Last night she asked him to bring the empty canning jars up from the basement, and the boxes are stacked in the corner. But it will be at least a month until she has any early tomatoes to occupy her time.

He comes into the kitchen smelling of soap, and in an instant she is surrounded by him. Please, she says, dinner, and she moves away.

Let me just kiss you, he says, and she turns around to face him. He is powerfully handsome, and unaware of it. He is good to her, loves her unquestioningly, and sometimes she wonders how to live to deserve love like this.

Sometimes she's afraid her love for him is not as great as his for her. She's afraid her weaker love is a slow poison.

There's a line of sunlight on the stone hearth like liquid fire. A gray cat green-eyed in the shadowed grass outside the kitchen window. Things take her by surprise. He's so very good to her, and she never wants to consciously be cruel to him. Maybe that's love enough to bind her here.

They eat dinner in front of the evening news, and things happening in other parts of the world determine the borders of their conversation. Years ago they discovered how pleasant this was, once a day turning outward, focusing their attention on Argentina or China. They talk easily. Now and then it bothers her that disasters happening to other people seem to bring them closer together and she'll wonder why they do this. One of them will come up with an explanation for it but no explanation seems to explain it fully. Sometimes it feels superstitious, knowing that the worst thing in the world that could happen is in fact happening someplace else reduces the chances of it happening here. As though there's a certain amount of evil and misery in the world and it's being used up in other places and can't touch them.

When the news is finished, she takes the plates into the kitchen and begins the dishes while he rests. He watches a re-run of a comedy. In the kitchen she can hear the hysteria of the laugh-track and none of the jokes. When she's done, she goes out to the garden, half-heartedly pulls a weed or two, checks the tomato plants for blossoms. She looks out over the fields, evidence of the way he's used his days.

Her plants grow on their own, haphazardly. Over the winter she had made plans for a perennial garden. She'd read books and made charts and ended up this spring one day sowing seeds and letting them fall where they did and grow how they would. Instead of the neat rising up and blooming of one plant and then another in sequence, she would have a week of clashing colors and two weeks or so with no flowers at all, when she couldn't tell the weeds from the plants.

She looks at the flowers now and has a vision of what she can do—thinning plants, moving things around for balance.

She hears the door to the house open and

then he is behind her, his arms around her again and she tenses for a second before she consciously relaxes. He kisses her hair and leans down to kiss her neck, and she leans back into him. He lets her go when he's ready and starts to head for the barn. She asks if she can help with anything, and he says not really. He says she should relax and enjoy this life before they have children. We'll both be busy when the children come.

She could separate those plants that are too close together. She could move out into the yard and pull them by the roots. But some days she feels as fragile as a pea. Fresh green, out of the pod, that soft skin that curls back like wood shavings.

He checks her temperature on this chart the doctor gave them. There is, it seems, a rhythm to her heat.

They try again in the evening and the next morning.

She lies on her back for hours after sex, just waiting. She puts her hips up on a pillow to make it easy. She thinks she should feel something when it happens. She thinks of white planes, those tiny bones rising out of an immense sky.

In the summer she comes alive. In the summer she remembers friends, remembers hobbies and projects. One summer she designed a quilt that won prizes, another summer hybridized a rose. (The bud she'd chosen for the female turned red, it swelled as the seeds ripened in the ovary. All the summer's work, the bags carefully covering the male and female, was wasted when in the fall she put the seeds in individual pots in her kitchen to grow into plants over the winter and by November she was busy with other things, and she let them die.)

And every summer for the past three years she's been pregnant for two months, and every fall the gravity has won out over her will.

Later in the morning she sits on the back step, rests her chin on her knees, brushes garden dirt from her legs. Her husband walks out of the barn carrying a metal container and a long hose and begins spraying a liquid over weeds growing along a fence by the corn. As soon as the poison hits them, they wilt; she knows that by morning they'll be a black that never occurs when they die naturally.

It's a strong poison that you can only use when the weeds are separate from things you really want to grow. He has others to use near the corn. A good farmer has to be a chemist. There's a railroad car outside the grain elevator, pouring pure white poison, smooth as sugar, into farmers' trucks.

She watches him put the canister back into the barn. He wipes his hands on the legs of his pants as he walks back toward her. It's dusk and she feels a rush of love for him, holds out her hand but he thrusts his hands back away from her, says Don't touch till I wash. She smiles, says Oh please, just a kiss, and he laughs, bends forward from the waist with his hands behind him and kisses her cheek. Now go wash, she says, and he laughs again and goes inside.

They turn on the television and hear that half the world is starving. They vow to send money, but somehow something happens — it's already cash in the pocket, or they owe it on bills, or they forget to mail the letter with the check and lose the address. She feels vaguely wrong every time she throws something away — the scraps off plates, grocery bags, plastic wrappers, each day's news, the broken appliances that aren't worth fixing. At the same time, the very same time, she wants to rip up the carpet in the living room because she's sick of it and wants to refinish the wood floor underneath, and once before when they did that she put the carpet out in the yard, close to the house in a roll, thinking they would take it to the Salvation Army, all good intentions, but soon forgot it, and there were a couple of rainstorms soaking it and eventually it went in the trash to be thrown away.

By this summer she could have had three

children. Some days she can feel where a baby should be in her arms.

Earlier in the morning, she told him. After lunch he's driving to the drugstore to buy this test they saw in a magazine. An hour after that, they'll know.

She walks around the kitchen, taking the tie from the bread, stripping the plastic back from the bologna. She notices that she's walking like a pregnant woman, her hips thrust forward, her hands on her back. She stops and walks into the bedroom, turns sideways and looks in the mirror. She's flushed from the sun and the heat. Maybe her eyes look different.

She hears him coming down the hallway. He treats her like husbands do on TV. He holds her stiff, like they were Ozzie and Harriet.

A hot breeze sucks the curtains against the screens. Dust swirls up and blows toward the garden. He relaxes, lifts her hair, kisses her neck. He puts his hand beneath her shirt, cups her belly like it's already round, draws circles with his finger. He looks so happy. She looks small to herself, her head low on his chest. His hands are twice as large as hers. He moves his hands up over her breasts. They feel like bruised fruit. She starts to cry.

He pulls back and strokes her hair, tells her to rest, that he'll finish lunch. She tells him she doesn't think she can eat. He smiles. You see, he says, I knew it would all turn out right.

She lies down on the bed. The magazine

showed this test tube with a red ring like the rim of the sun. She hears him rustling around the kitchen, his car fading as he backs out of the driveway and down the road.

In August she begins canning. She puts up quarts of tomatoes. The kitchen is filled with steam, a shelf in the basement lined with red jars. The second week he brings in a bushel of apples and she peels and cooks them, adds cinnamon, a row of applesauce next to the tomatoes. The third week she's canning beans, with bushels of zucchini waiting. By the end of August she's peeling pear-shaped tomatoes yellow as egg yolks. She makes zucchini relish and zucchini pickles. He's brought in three bushels of cucumbers which she cuts into slices and puts in crocks, the kitchen rich with the yeast smell of dill. There are hills of potatoes ready to dig and onions drying on the steps, bell peppers heaped on the counter by the sink, still more bushels of apples until, he was right, she's working from early morning until late evening, giddy with the harvest, and by Labor Day it's been three months and she's begun to hope.

By the second week in September she's through canning. Often in the afternoons she goes down into the basement to lean against the cool walls and look at the brightly colored jars. She stands there afraid to move, or she sits on the back step or on the couch. He is even more gentle to her, even more kind. They begin to lose interest in the news and they sit together in the evening with the TV off, talking. A tension around his eyes and jaws that she'd never noticed before disappears; she only sees its absence.

In October the fields turn the color of bone. The chrysanthemums bloom. The harvest is ripe, and he has to work past midnight. There's a single light on the front of the combine, slashing through the corn.

At night he comes in the house and leaves his clothes in the mudroom for her to wash. They're slick with dust. They smell strongly of machine oil. He takes a shower and comes out wrapped in a towel. He sits beside her on the bed, strokes her hair, runs his thumb along her cheekbone. We're so lucky, he says. Good things happen to us. We make them happen.

He lays his head on her chest. His dark hair is slightly damp. He runs his hand down her swollen stomach, says this is what I live for, this will make it all seem real.

She feels the first cramps in the late afternoon as she's washing one of his shirts. At first it's slight, possible to think it doesn't feel like the last time. It's a hot day for October.

He comes in for supper and she screams at him for tracking mud. After they eat, he goes back out in the dark.

She sits in a lawn chair by the hardy asters. She watches his blade cut the bleached corn. He stays, as always, one row ahead of the frost, dreaming of the harvest.

in the john dillinger museum

A man and a woman are walking down the street, and they pause in front of the John Dillinger Museum. Was this John Dillinger's house? the woman asks, and the man, who knows things, says no, that Dillinger was from up around Mooresville. But it doesn't matter, he says; to the right of the house is the Joan Crawford birdbath, and Joan never set foot in Indiana.

All up and down the street tourists are buying calico and ceramic ducks. Artists sit in retirement studios cranking out their visions of the surrounding hills. Centuries ago glaciers wrinkled up the land like the skin of a hound and left this hollow down somewhere near the belly for people to set up gift shops and amusements.

Behind the John Dillinger Museum a man in his fifties plays a guitar with no finish, and now and then he accompanies himself on the kazoo. He plays all day long for change. Earlier, the woman and the man sat on a bench eating ice cream and listening to him play. They left him a dollar. The guitar player lives for his music, in a camper behind the food store. In the mornings he practices and watches teenagers in shorts and thongs walk in and out of the store, sucking on thin-necked bottles of Coke. He is always in love but has never married. The woman is afraid her husband envies what he fancies is the man's much simpler life.

Next to the John Dillinger Museum is a toy shop. The owner dips a long stick into a bucket of soap suds. He makes bubbles as large as a six-year-old. The bubbles are heavy and irregular with the weight of their own iridescent skins. They lumber and sag through the air and rise up right before their spark-filled burst. He can only make one bubble at a

time. One creeps around the corner of the museum and explodes near the woman's eyes. For
a moment the air is filled with soapy glitter,
like silky microscopic seeds.

So what say we go in the John Dillinger
Museum? says the man, her husband who
knows things. On a day like this? she wants to
say. Spend it in a dark museum? She wants to
keep walking toward dinner, a table in a light-
filled window. But she can tell by the way he
looks so hungrily at the picture of a wax Dillinger all laid out in the morgue that this trip is
not a negotiable one. A spiral notepad and a
pen are stuffed in the shirt pocket where her father, she remembers, kept his cigarettes.

The man's face is starting to wrinkle in
that flat space in front of his ears. Time is passing quickly. His father's skin folded in the same
way; she knows exactly what he'll look like
twenty years from now. His skin is dark olive.
Some of his ancestors were Mediterranean. He
knows all about his ancestors. Her knowledge
of the past stops with her grandparents; beyond that it's a primal fog. It seems to her that
that's the way it should be. He's always trying
to trace the tangled threads of personality back
through generations.

It doesn't matter. Though she hates the
thought of going inside the John Dillinger Museum, she'll go. She'll get through it somehow,
all those wax faces staring at her all unblinking

and unresponsive, the scary way they always seem to breathe if you stare at them for long, like her grandmother who winked at her from the coffin. Her mother said it must have been the very moment that her soul left her body. When you look at a human face, it should respond to you, not sit there silent and brooding as a tree.

Wax figures always look like dead people, she says to her husband, and he says yes, I guess that's why they're fascinating, like you want to pare the waxy crayon flesh with your fingers to see what's underneath.

They walk up on the porch and he stands there reading every word on the posters designed to attract him inside. "I could have spent hours; it was worth every penny"—a quote from some nameless woman in Cincinnati. She watches his lips move as he reads, his eyes wide with hunger. "Offered without social or moral comment," another poster says, "the Dillinger Museum is dedicated to the loss and sorrow on both sides of the law."

The Dillinger Museum is a barn-red house with white gingerbread trim, a good house for selling quilts or woven placemats. She turns around to look at the quaint street, the white picket fence they passed through. If it were up to her, she'd strip the house of its wax and fake blood and Joan Crawford birdbath and she'd put up a porch swing or a rocker, one of those where the twigs are soaked in water and then gently bent into shape, not forced or pounded. She would sit on this porch then and not read a word, just sit and watch the people stream by—every year a different clothing fad, every year a different purchase, but always the ice cream and the soft drinks and the lovers and the young families all weary from hiking, and the old couples holding hands. It seems to her that everywhere she looks there's a harmony, an intimacy she's lost or somehow never found: the comfort of families who are parts of the same whole, and they're the only two people who live in dissonance and grating, the daily misunderstandings which have led them here to the John Dillinger Museum where he wants to go in and she just wants to sit on the porch in a pure untinctured state, with all the worries and the differences between them boiled away so they'll always be as peaceful and alike as two glasses of distilled water. Now and then they'd clink at the hip in this bell-like ringing, and they'd pour their thoughts from one to the other and merge so completely you could never tell the difference between them. Instead, they're cups of liquid struck so hard from the outside that the circles travel inward, and refuse to touch.

I'll bet you could spend hours in here, her husband says, quoting the kindred spirit woman from Cincinnati, and he leads her through the door. A sign inside assures visitors that the machine guns behind glass are all reproductions, that the snub-nose 38 pointing straight at them in the wax Clyde's hand, Bonnie languishing on a chair at his feet, has no bullets, that even if you smashed the glass you couldn't shoot a soul.

A woman sits behind a bank teller's cage, bored as a zoo animal. She's in a bank no one would ever rob. She hands them a card for their money. No pictures, no food. There are four rooms. Children and people with weak hearts or other organs are advised to skip room three.

So, she says, this is the John Dillinger Museum. I guess if you live your life cruelly enough, someone will celebrate it.

I know, her husband says. Soon there'll be a Jim Jones Museum and a Charlie Manson Museum and a D. C. Stephenson Museum in among the apple butter shops.

Except that Dillinger wasn't really cruel, he adds, he was just a thief. There are all sorts of people around here who helped him hide. To some of them, he was a hero.

Oh, he was cruel, she thinks. Dillinger was a sharp metal edge pulling at the tight threads of the smooth midwestern grid, hammering the strings of banks and perfect homes like his own personal piano. He stole over a million dollars in fourteen months, a million l930s dollars from families just trying to get by. Depression dollars. At least those families had someone specific and evil to blame for their suffering, she thinks. You could hate Dillinger, hate him clear through.

You can see why women loved him, she overhears a woman saying to the man she's with. Look at that dark hair, and those eyes.

Silly fool, she thinks, and she looks away from the woman and over at a yellowed poster on the wall. It states up front that this is not Dillinger's house but that he once robbed a grocery store an hour north. The sign also says that the TV movie is a pitiful poor excuse for a movie. The real truth about Dillinger, the sign says, is right here in this house.

Room One is small and cluttered with things. There are mirrors beside each window to make the room seem larger. Her own reflection takes her by surprise. The light is too gray. She looks older than she thought, and tired. So does her husband. She wants him to see what she sees. They'll never have another child. But he doesn't see himself; he's looking at the pictures of the white farmhouse that was Dillinger's childhood home. Dillinger's family stares back at her husband with that early depression dust-bowl seriousness. In every picture in her own photo album she and her husband have those giddy camera smiles. If their photos were ever on a wall like this with all the other families from this time and place, it would look like Eden—like a time of great tranquillity and happiness.

Dillinger was a chubby child. His parents loved him, or so it seemed from the photographs. She doesn't understand why he couldn't leave well enough alone, take the fate his life had given him. The poverty of that farmhouse couldn't be wished away. There was a straight line to follow between any two points. You don't just try to leap into some new dimension.

She looks around for something to pull her away from the thing she feels she's getting too close to—which is what?—Dillinger's childhood and the peaceful farm and the mother and the father, a glass case filled with wood and metal 1920s toys. Not his toys of course but the kind of toys he might have played with, and this the magazine he might have read, and this the brand of food he might have eaten, none of them adding up to the explosion of newsprint on the opposite wall screaming *robbery, robbery*, oh why did he have to bring her here on this sunny day to the John Dillinger Museum?

She looks out the window. A woman walks by outside in a yellow dress; behind her, a mother pushes a stroller. All these people walking by, not turning in the gate, with no idea what waits for them inside. Please hurry, she says to him, please. This room should only take a second to see. You could stand in the center and turn and see it all, but he pauses at each article, reads every word, wonders at each metal toy, each driftwood graying wooden block, as though it were all a puzzle that his life depended on. If their lives were arranged in a house like this would it all make as little sense as this place did? Nothing could change the past, it's best to leave it all alone, and still he went back and back to it, trying to understand.

He won't write anything down, she knows, until after he's out of the building, and then he'll do it almost guiltily, as though it's something he's ashamed of. He'll continue talking to her, but he'll be lost in his own thoughts, and it will be hours before she can reclaim him. And in the morning, early, he'll be up there again in the spare bedroom, adding pages to that pile of typed pages that's been growing for months, thinking that the John Dillinger Museum could be the key to finally unlock all those miles and miles of solitary thoughts.

He looks over at her and smiles. He can tell she's bored or uncomfortable, and he tries hard to pretend that he thinks the museum is silly. He comments on the overwrought signs and the Dillinger T-shirts displayed in every room; he wants her to believe they're living in the same world still, though she knows he's gone already, flying out over some crevice like a spider with a sticky thread, and she's the wall he wants to stay attached to, the hand holding the weaving kite. Where do you go? she wants to shout at him. Why do you leave me here alone like this?

She takes his arm and feels the warmth of his blood; she wants to hear it speak to her. Are you there? Are you still with me?

They walk into Room Two. More wax figures. Ma Barker wears a purple coat. Except for the machine gun, she looks like anybody's mother. Carbines line the wall, this room an arsenal.

A waxy Pretty Boy Floyd stands with his back to a window. She could have seen him from outside, right from where they'd been sitting earlier, watching the guitar player.

This room is hot. It smells like candles. They should be sitting down to dinner now. She would have a glass of wine, dark red as a garnet. It would be the two of them alone, the waiter faceless. They would watch the sun leave, the town get dusky dark. Firelight would glint on the white plates, on the yellow grain in the wooden floor. They would float there, alone, above a white tablecloth, the two of them, and when she looked at him she would know exactly who it was she was looking at. She realizes that she doesn't really trust him. She wants to trust him, but he's become complicated and moody and contradictory, and the harder he tries not to be, the worse it is. When he says that he loves her, she doesn't have any idea in the world what that means to him.

She looks down at the case beside her. Inside is a wooden gun carved out of the top board of a washtub. It's more clunky than the roughest toy. It's the gun, she reads, that Dillinger used to escape from the Lake County prison. It's the pride of the museum. Underneath it is a letter typed on yellow paper by Dillinger himself. It's long and chatty, and the ribbon needed changing.

Dear Sis! Dillinger writes. *Here's the gun they thought was real!* he writes. The letter is filled with Ha! Ha!'s like any ordinary boy's. *Keep it for me,* he tells his sister. *Twelve big prison guards locked up because of this wooden gun, ha ha. Look at it when you need a good laugh,* he says. *Ha! Ha! Love, Johnny.*

It's a silly, childish gun. It shouldn't fool a soul. He must have been a magician; he had to believe in that wooden gun. He had to get the guards to see it in his face, to keep their eyes away from that splintery stick of wood in his hand.

Across the room, her husband leans so close to a case that she can see his breath on the glass. A handsome Dillinger stands staring at him from the other side. Blue whiskers like flecks of metal in his pale face. Her husband's reflection floats above Dillinger's dark suit; Dillinger's hat rests on her husband's watery head. His hand reaches out toward the case and she's afraid she sees Dillinger's arm rising, and for a dizzy second it looks as though they're touching.

She runs from the room and feels her husband follow her. Only two more rooms, he says, his breath against her cheek. She won't look at him. He's a complete stranger to her. Nothing he can learn will bring their son back; there's nothing they can do. She wishes she were married to an accountant, a man who would leave for work on time in a three-piece suit, someone who remembered to record the checks, to pay the bills, a man whose loyalty is to the world that you can see, a man who would know how to deal with tragedy.

They wind up the narrow stairs. Photographs of the Midwest in the thirties line the stairwell. Hollow eyes, rusted gas tanks collapsing on themselves like cloth, barns falling from their own weight. Thirties honky-tonk plays cheerfully on the loud speakers. Oh please come with me, she turns and whispers to him, and it's the young innocent boy she married that she says it to, the one who's been replaced by this private, suffering man. I'm here, he says, and he puts his hand on her shoulder, but he doesn't really see her.

I'm hungry, she says to him, just to hear

her normal voice. Just two more rooms, he says, and she mentions a place down the street with fried chicken and biscuits, a place that's never changed in all the years they've been coming here, a place that smells, always, of sassafras tea.

There are warnings outside of Room Three. Don't come in! it says, if you're faint-hearted. Go on to Room Four! Her husband walks right in. The warning's not for her, she thinks, and she follows him inside.

There are pictures of the Biograph and of the woman who lured him in. This is the truth about John Dillinger, the poster says, not the movie truth. The lady in red? Her dress was really orange. The movie he went to see was a comedy. The woman wasn't his girlfriend, just an acquaintance who wanted $3,000. Here are pictures of all the women he loved; the woman in orange wasn't one of them.

The honky-tonk music fades out in this room, is replaced by the sound of gunfire and squealing tires. All the G-men in the world stare out at her, and wait to gun Dillinger down.

She looks up at a clear plastic Invisible Man sculpture of Dillinger's head. A red plastic arrow is embedded in his cheek, underneath the eye. It won't be enough to see the body and the blood. This is how it will happen. This is the place that death will enter in.

She thinks of Dillinger's mother's face in the photographs downstairs. She wonders if she suffered for her son, if she thought of all the sons who suffered because of the child she'd given life to.

Oh, this room is the one she's waited for. This room is the way it should be. This room is the serious room, the moral room, the one that comes with warnings. It may have looked like excitement, the room cries, but after all the women and the drinking and the banks ripe and splitting open like a pod, and all the mothers in the world and all the fathers suffering for their sons and for their daughters, this is what it comes to in the end: Dillinger stone cold on a slab, crayon blood dripping eternally down his eternally contorted face, a facsimile of the wicker basket they carried him in underneath the table. This is what she needed to see, what her husband needs to see. She leans into his shoulder, walks with him from picture to picture like any couple at a gallery. Dillinger's public execution, the expression on the bystanders' faces óne common face of horror and of fascination.

These are the real blood-stained trousers, this is his face contorted in anguish. This is the room you can be angry in, the one where Dillinger is murdered over and over in photograph after photograph. His is the face you want to smash, and here is the scream that waits in your throat for the moment it can rise up clear and clean to the edges of the universe, the defiant *no*, the *why*, your fist finding its home, finally, in Dillinger's white and perfect teeth.

And still, somehow, it's not enough. They head into the final room. She looks at her husband's face to see if here in the John Dillinger Museum he can see what she's afraid of, how treacherous the road they're on.

Room Four regrets the passion. Calmly, the room says that it isn't right, revenge that hot and sudden. It won't do. It leaves you cold. The room shifts suddenly to the Lindbergh baby thief. This is his room. Here's the real revenge, the room says, Hauptmann with his weasel face sitting in the electric chair, the slow rational burn the only satisfaction. Dillinger should have died this way but didn't. By comparison, Dillinger in his satin coffin, fresh from a comedy, is peaceful, about to wake from sleep. Hauptmann has the look of a man who's seen the wrong, a man who knows he's going to die.

She stares at Hauptmann's face. She stares and stares at it. The room is windowless and cold. They've been in here too long. There's nothing for them here, no explanations.

Her husband turns away from her and heads back down the stairs and out the door. She runs behind him.

Outside, a man is playing a kazoo. Outside, the day is clear and filled with sun. Some-one's hanging wind chimes on a clothesline. Her husband's eyes are lonely as a child's. Whatever is behind those eyes is dark and hid-den.

They're pulled into the rush of people on the sidewalk. She holds on to his hand like the string of a kite. Please, she says as he begins to fly away from her, don't leave me here alone in the John Dillinger Museum.

p r i s o n e r s

*We are persuaded that a thread
runs through all things: all
worlds are strung on it, as
beads; and men, and events, and
life, come to us only because of
that thread.*

— Emerson

i

There were several large ships in the middle of Pearl Harbor when the bombs began to fall, fifty years ago today. One of the ships was lit for a party; there was a band on board, and you could hear the music on the shore.

As the ship went down, the hold filled rapidly with water. But there was a bubble of air up high, enough for hundreds of trapped men to breathe in.

It was a shallow harbor. The ship was armor plated, five inches or more of metal, and it was impossible at that time to drill through and rescue them.

The old men on television remembered

hearing the trapped men screaming—at night when they were on patrol or just walking along the shore. They told how they stuffed cotton in their ears, but it didn't block the sound.

The screaming went on from December 7 to December 23 until, blessedly, it stopped. And you could walk along the shore in silence.

i i

The old jail looks like any Victorian museum—red brick with white gingerbread. The kids go crazy with corn dogs and lemonade, with face paint and hula hoops. Underneath a tent, teenagers are modeling 100-year-old lace dresses and tarnished suits. Men and women sit in rows like obedient teacups. There's a German oom pah band and a middle-aged woman dressed like a gypsy. She'll tell your fortune for a quarter. The day's too hot, the sky's a slick enamel blue.

We buy tickets to see the jail, and we stand in line waiting our turn. I've come with my friend Julie, her three children, and my two. Please, my son is saying, I don't want to go in. He's too young to stay outside by himself, and we've driven all this way, so I try to reassure and cajole him. He's afraid that we'll all be locked inside. That won't happen, I promise him. We haven't done anything wrong. We're not bad people.

Maybe on accident, he says.

All the police and all the firemen and all the ministers and all the king's horses would come with torches and hammers to let us out, I say. It doesn't help. If we see that we're going into a place with a lock on it, I say, we'll just stand back and watch, OK? We won't go in.

He says that's OK and that afterward he wants some french fries. Done, I tell him.

They let a group of people out of jail and send the next group in.

We're let in through an ordinary Victorian parlor. There are gilt-framed pictures and over-stuffed chairs and a lot of lace. Did the prisoners come in this way? I ask, and the guide says no, that there was a side door for the prisoners. This front part was where the sheriff lived with his wife and family. The wife and children and the family guests never had to see the prisoners if they didn't want to. The husband would always be on call.

We walk through the parlor and down a hall lined with yellowed newspaper clippings. We turn right, down a set of stairs.

It's cool in the basement, and dark. It smells like rusted metal. The guide takes us through a room with a furnace and an old voting machine. Estes Kefauver, whoever he is, is eternally running for president. Then he takes us back to a square stone-walled room. Most of the center of the room is taken up by large pipes. Above our heads, resting on ball bearings on a circular track and on one giant column in the center of the basement, we see the bottom of what will turn out to be a large metal cylinder, two stories high, like a gigantic tin can. From 1881 until 1973 this was the Montgomery County Jail.

It's Labor Day, the day before school starts. All three of Julie's children have red hair like her husband's. They look like three unlit matches standing in front of us. Julie is blonde, one of those calm, patient mothers that you see waiting in line at planetariums and children's museums. On the phone, the day before, Julie had been crying.

Sometimes I think I'm a crummy mother, she had said, just such a crummy mother.

You're a great mother, I told her, you love those kids.

No I'm not, she said. You don't know.

So tell me, I said.

And it went something like this: *Lexey's been having these tantrums, completely irrational ones like children have—I don't want it to rain or something that she can't control, and it escalates. It's the age she is, everything is me me. A few weeks ago she hit a little boy with a ball bat, not hard enough to hurt him thank*

God, but she had a tantrum when I tried to send her to her room because she couldn't understand why she couldn't hit him if he was in her way, but he was in my WAY she kept screaming, he was in my way—and especially if there are neighborhood children in the house, and they're all talking at once. I have my own things I'm thinking about, and maybe we're in a hurry to go someplace and I hear this shrill witchy voice come out of my mouth. For hours I'll be patient, patient, and then suddenly I'll snap—Get in the car! I'll yell, for no real reason, she doesn't understand where it's coming from all of the sudden, Get in the car! And what I'm thinking is even worse, it's murderous. I figured it out once, and when we're all at home someone is saying Mom this and Mom that every four seconds on an average. It's all Bach, all simultaneous, and I'm thinking that this is my one and only adult life I'm living and I can't think enough to get it straight and in my mind I'm screaming at them to get in the car, get in the fucking car. Sometimes I'm afraid I really will snap. I feel like a witch sometimes, such an unbelievable witch.

You're one of the most patient mothers I've ever seen, I said. And she is, very loving and patient.

Then why don't I feel it, she said, why do I feel so knotted up?

You're too hard on yourself, I said.

People say that, they say I'm a good mother, but I swear to God I'm not even half-way close to decent. When I'm away from the kids they're with me all the time like phantom limbs—there's no one in the world I love more than those kids—but since they were born it feels like I've had absolutely no white space, that every minute we're awake together belongs to them, and I know I could say no, I want to read go play or no, I'm talking to a friend go play, but it doesn't work. They stand there and they keep on talking, and with three of them one is always in danger or always in a fight—last week a neighbor boy bit my son on the stomach the same day Lexey hit her friend with a baseball bat the same day another neighbor shot the garage door window with a b-b gun the same day Lexey's other little friend Allison was crying to go home because she missed her mother when I'd promised to baby-sit for two hours. Sometimes when I go to sleep at night my teeth are chattering I'm so tired, it has nothing to do with cold.

The guide's a retired man with white hair and papery skin. He leans against the wall and tells stories, but his voice is soft and only the three or so people who are standing next to him—men and women in their early sixties, that age when you suddenly become fascinated with history—can hear what he's saying, and they're all excited and asking questions. Now and then we hear one of the questions and infer by the direction the old man's pointing what the answer is. What we're looking at, it seems, is the plumbing. The pipes gather waste from the cells and siphon it off into the ground.

Julie's older son works his way up near the guide, and he comes back with information. This thing weighs 54,000 pounds, he says, but you can turn it with thirteen pounds of force on a single crank. It's an amazing machine. Two guys from Indianapolis invented it; they even got a patent. Eventually they built seventeen of these things, but this is the only one that still turns.

There it goes, he says, and it does. It creaks and turns in a complete and easy circle right above our heads.

Can you believe there used to be people in there? my son asks as we head up the stairs. On Friday I'll bet you got dizzy as hell, my friend says, all the drunks coming in, the jail turning every hour or so.

We go through a metal door and into the three-story-high square room that houses the jail. The jail turns like a carousel inside the room. See, I tell my son, they won't let us into the cells. They ask us to stand against the walls, in the part of the jail that would be, if you were cutting out a pie crust, the part of the

dough you would throw away. The cells themselves are shaped like pieces of pie, with a pipe
and a toilet at the point in the center. There are
no sinks, just a shower head in the wall we're
leaning against, and grates on the floor for the
water. The bunks are made of steel and are too
short for anyone to stretch out on. The outer
crust of the pie is a ring of bars. The pieces turn
inside the crust inside the room. There's only
one opening, and to get a prisoner in or out, or
in order for the prisoner to get his food, the
whole jail has to turn until the cell you need is
in front of the opening. It's like that opening
on a round packet of needles, the one you turn
until you find the needle you want. Then you
shake it out into your hand.

The attractive thing about this design was
that the jailer never had to come in contact
with a prisoner, not even to give him food.
There was a pass-through slit in the outer wall.
You just spun the jail around until the prisoner
fell out into the outer section, and you pushed
the food in to him. He'd go back into his cell,
and then you'd spin the jail around again. It
was a complete system, the grand unified theory of jails. On a stairway landing between the
first and second floors there were two station-
ary cells for mental patients. The toilets and
sinks were made from cast iron with no remov-
able parts that prisoners could break off or
harm themselves with. The rotating jail is two

stories high. The third floor is a large square room with a wooden floor and large windows. It feels like a ballroom. There are two small barred cells built into the middle, very much like cages. These were for women prisoners.

We're led back out again through the parlor. We're glad when we get out into the sunlight and the heat. Out here it's a festival, a day of celebration. Steven gets his french fries, her son goes to have his fortune told, the girls pick up hula hoops and swirl them on their hips. They condemned the jail in 1973. I was graduating from college that year, an hour away from here, and I had no idea it existed.

i i i

There's something temporary, permeable, about the word *jail,* a lightness the word *prison* doesn't have. A prison is a complete world which turns, hidden, inside the outer world. A jail is a bus station, an airport, a place where you wait until you're flung back into your old life or forward to some new one. People sink into a prison, they disappear, and the world weaves a seamless cloth behind them.

The malls were filled with too many people, and with too much noise. Those of us who'd stayed away from them felt trapped inside our houses. Those of us who'd ventured out felt trapped by too much glittering choice.

In the mall we walked past aisles and aisles of jewel-toned sweaters and dresses, past cellophane-wrapped toys. We saw pieces of ourselves reflected in hat and shoe and suit department mirrors, on china plates and aluminum toasters, on the circular chrome racks of sale blouses. (And the disconcerting five-inch version that appeared from out of nowhere on television screens, the one that walked beside us for a foot or two and then veered off, lost out of range of the hidden camera.) We watched people handing clerks their plastic cards and then saying "well now I've taken care of him. Now I've got *that* one off my list." That's the kind of day it had been. It had been that kind of day. Something felt off balance, and we weren't sure what or why. It was misty, gray December. The beginning of flu season.

In the evening, twelve of us gathered in the cold outside the entrance to the Indiana Women's Prison. We had a truck full of cookies and punch mix, boxes of gift saltwater taffy, licorice, and hair spray. We waited for the guards to let us in.

One or two of us were coughing. We were all volunteers. We didn't know each others'

names, and by the end of the evening, we still
wouldn't know them.

"I've never been here before," I said to the
man standing beside me. "Neither have I," he
said. The man looked eager. "Around Thanksgiving," he said, "my wife and I wanted to do
something for someone, and we called all over
the city, thinking we could sling some hash.

"But no one needed us — not the homeless,
not the mentally ill."

"They always need people in the prisons,"
a woman said. "I was here last year. There's
something about that heavy metal door shut-
ting behind you that terrifies a lot of people."

I looked at the twelve-foot fences and the
large glinting hoops of metal on top of them. It
was prettier than barbed wire, looked like
yards of silvery ribbon candy. "It's razor
sharp," the woman said. She had a red Christmas bulb hanging from each earlobe. "Sometimes people will throw coats over the top of
them and maybe get in or out, but it happens
rarely."

I'd spent the day inside, baking cookies
with my kids. I brought four dozen here and
had six dozen at home waiting for a cookie exchange party the next day. Earlier, when I'd
told my friend Alice I was coming out here to
serve cookies at the prison Christmas party,
she'd said that the women's prison had never

once crossed her mind. It never occurred to her to wonder if there was one, or if there was, where it could be. I told her it was downtown, just a little southeast of Market Square. "I've lived in this city all my life," she said, "my whole entire life, and I've never seen or heard of it."

I'd passed it once, I told her, when I had a speeding ticket and had to go to court out on Raymond Street. It was a speed-trap speeding ticket I got the last month I was pregnant with Laura. Somehow I forgot to pay the fine and a couple of months later had to go out to this small municipal court in a strip mall. I'd driven by the Women's Prison then, but somehow didn't really register that it was there. There are a lot of small factories out that way, and it just looked like one of those.

I remembered how furious I'd been when I got the ticket. I was nine months pregnant, going thirty-five in a thirty-mile-an-hour zone, a policeman was hiding in a driveway and flagging whole flotillas of us down. I was innocent, a good person, I had a good job and a regular family; couldn't he see by my smile that we were on the same side?

"If there is a women's prison," Alice said, "don't you imagine that they're all in there because they got in with one bad-news guy or another, someone who told them to do something they never would have thought of themselves?"

I had no idea, hadn't given much thought to the women's prison either. I thought it would be like TV or some lower circle of hell: that the women would look hard and they would look like they were suffering. I pictured them wearing prison scrubs. It was the last place in the world I could imagine myself being.

A guard let us in and directed us to the recreation hall. We walked across what looked like a college quadrangle—a large expanse of green surrounded by brick dormitories. At the end of the quadrangle there was a brick build-ing with a steeple and palladium windows, like a church. Inside, a linoleum floor, chairs, a small stage, weight-lifting equipment pushed against the wide walls. Church services on Sunday, aerobics on the weekdays.

There were three women waiting for us. One was a woman in late-middle age. For a while I thought she was another volunteer, but this was her job. She had the short temper of self-inflicted martyrdom. The other two wom-en wore badges like telephone linemen, and street clothes. For a while I assumed they were guards or some kind of aides. "The ones with photo badges are all prisoners," a volunteer told me.

We started to unload the truck. "You don't need to do that," the matron said, "the girls will do it for you." But we shrugged our shoulders and kept unloading.

When we got the boxes in, we began taking cookies out of Christmas tins and putting them on plastic trays. "Your hands!" the matron shouted, "Your hands!"

"I think we're supposed to wear gloves," one of the women said. "Why?" another woman asked. "We have clean hands. The women in my church made twelve hundred of these cookies. Two or three people have touched every one of them already, what difference does it make?"

"Food service rules," the matron said, and she called the infirmary and asked them to send over plastic gloves.

Two of the volunteers were nuns from a monastery in Beech Grove. In the Sunday paper there had been an article about how they were a dying breed. "All this sugar," one of the nuns said, "look at all the sugar. Wouldn't it have been better to bring healthy things, like maybe carrot sticks or salads?"

We got the gloves and went back to sorting cookies onto round trays. Our hands no longer felt like our hands. The cookies felt like plastic.

One of the prisoners came over beside us. "Can I help?" she asked. "We're just about done," a woman said. Already several of us were standing around feeling useless.

The prisoner was a small woman, about 5'3", with a beautiful face and eyes, and short dark hair. When she smiled, the corner of her mouth shook. There was a film of cloudy liquid over her eyes. Later, when all the prisoners came in, I would see other women like that, beautiful young women on the verge of tears. One was wearing a burgundy loose-fitting dress. She had long dark hair down to her waist.

The prisoner with glossy eyes talked to us. We find out that her children are nine and eleven; she sees them, if the father will bring them, once or twice a year. "That's been the hardest thing," she said. Many of the women will say that during the evening. Most of them have children. "About 80 percent of them do," a guard said. "And I'd say three-fourths of them have custody."

"Who's taking care of the kids?" I asked her.

"Grandparents mostly. In only about 10 percent of the cases it's a spouse or boyfriend."

The guards came in leading a line of 200 women. They stood in line waiting to fill napkins with cookies. When the cookies were gone we'd bring out gift bags of taffy and red licorice and there would be something heartbreaking about it all, like it's something only chil-

dren should do, and even then, there's
something heartbreaking about children lined
up for recess or for lunch.

"This is not at all what I expected," one of
the nuns said to me, and I agreed, it wasn't.
The women looked no different, absolutely not
one bit different from any randomly put together group of Indiana women.

Or rather, it looked like any randomly put
together group of Indiana people. "There
are men in here," the nun said. "Look at that
guy," she said, and she pointed to a woman
who had the mannerisms of an adolescent
male down cold—the baseball cap on backward, the way she moved her shoulders and
her hips. It was a perfect parody, the one surreal touch. There was a white woman in her
early sixties who looked exactly like any
woman her age that you'd see in a small-town
meeting of the Eastern Star or local civil de-
fense. She had a white nylon jacket, reddish-
tinted gray bouffant hair, a round matronly
stomach. Sitting on the chair next to her was
her husband, and she looked exactly the way
she should as well—baggy blue jeans, gray
T-shirt over a beer belly, slicked back gray Elvis
hair.

"I've worked with women," the guard
said, "who bound their breasts so tight it was
medieval. There was a woman who would

point her shoes the right way when she uri-
nated, facing the wall, the way a man's
would."

"Do these relationships last?" the nun
asked.

"A lot of them," she said. "Their relationships with men were so appallingly horrible
that anything is better. Over half of them have
been abused. For most of these women, prison
is much safer."

The women sat listening to the jazz band
on the stage like any group of people listening
to music: young couples in love with their arms
draped around one another, older, more sedate
couples quietly holding hands.

"You know, there's something sort of
wonderful about that guy," one of the volunteers said to me, and I looked over to where
she was pointing to a woman in her early thirties, a woman with absolutely no trace of conventional femininity. And I said yes, there's
something fascinating about him, and we
tried to figure out what it was. He's good-looking, we agreed, but not a caricature like some
of the others. He's quiet, we decided, seems
unconflicted or wise or something. Strong.
"Like if the building were burning down," she
said, "he would oh gosh know how to save
us."

"That's not quite it," the woman said. She

had a red Christmas tree light necklace and tole-painted wooden earrings. "It's that he respects women."

The girlfriend's gorgeous but shallow, we decided. Not good enough for him. "As soon as she gets out of here," a prisoner who was standing near us said, "it's goodbye and forget I ever knew you." At the end of the evening, when they went to their separate dorms, they looked like any college couple saying good-bye—the guy maybe a year or two older, more experienced and protective of her, absolutely trustworthy. I love you, the girl said, and she cried as she left the rec hall. I love you, he whispered—a strong, silent, fifties male. And of course he didn't cry.

I talked to a woman with three children. She was serving the tenth year of her sentence. She'd been in this place since she was in her early thirties. "What keeps you sane?" I asked her. "My children do," she said, "thinking about them, knowing they're safe."

She'd been married twice, and both husbands beat her. She found out that the second husband was sexually abusing her daughter and one day, when she saw him talking to her, she snapped and shot him. "Couldn't you prove you were defending your children?" I asked. "It doesn't matter," the woman said. "Do the children know you were sacrificing yourself for them?" "Yes," the woman said, "they know and we get along fine. They write me."

I asked a guard about her. "She's a good woman," he said, "a real good woman. Some of the women had a lot of provocation for killing the guy. And anyway," he said, "murderers are the most stable group in a prison population." The majority of murders are part of the tangled relationship between two people. Outside the relationship, it seems, they manage fine.

"Can't she get out early on parole?" I asked. "Nobody gets out early," the guard said, "not any more.

"Ever since the last presidential election when Dukakis got in all that trouble. Governors aren't granting it to anyone anymore. Especially Bayh. He wants to run for president and doesn't want some inmate spoiling it for him."

A woman came out of the crowd to where I was standing with another volunteer. She was a heavy woman, wore a simple skirt and blouse, had curly brown hair. You could imagine her in a suit, working at a bank—the way she smiled at us, and started making small talk. She looked us directly in the eyes. She shook our hands. Whatever it is that prisoners show on their faces—a humility or fear or shame or anger—whatever it is that allows you to say "that one's a prisoner and that one's a guard" even before you see the badge—didn't show on her face.

She apologized for the way she looked. "I've gained eighty pounds since I've been here," she said. "I usually don't look this way." And I was right—she used to work as a bank manager. "It's hard for me to be here," she said. "There's no one I can really talk to."

She found out that the other volunteer worked in a job-training program, and she asked for advice. "I'm used to good jobs," she said, "and I'm afraid that with this on my record I won't be able to find one."

It was like talking with a neighbor. We talked weather, we talked Christmas baking, we talked clothes and family.

"It's really not as awful in here as I thought though," she said, "not as bad as Central State. My lawyer plea-bargained for me, and I got five years. I chose Central State first, but it was so much worse."

I asked her if she read about the patient who froze to death there a few days before. She said she hadn't heard, what happened?

"Stupid window was frozen open eighteen inches, and with all the psych drugs in her system, and below-freezing temperatures, she just froze.

"People had made requests to have that window repaired for months, one of the aides had looked in on her an hour before she died, it was just purely stupid. This state puts no

money into mental health; it's like we don't believe in mental illness, we think it's something
caused by lack of character."

"Conditions in the prisons are a little better," she said, "believe it or not. I've seen both
of them now."

"What did you do to get in here?" I asked. I
found out later that I was violating some sort of
protocol by asking, but she didn't seem to mind.

She looked directly at me. "I shot my
eight-month-old baby," she said.

"I get depressed," she told us, "psychotic.
I hear voices, get crazy ideas that I have complete faith in. I'm fine when I'm medicated, like
now, but I had to go off my medication when I
got pregnant, and I went into a post-partum
psychosis. I thought people were coming after
the baby, that they were going to kill us both. I
thought I was protecting her.

"I shot her face off," she said to us. "My
lawyer said that any jury, looking at those pictures, would give me life. So we made the plea
bargain, and here I am.

"The drugs I'm on now, it's like I'm floating above it all in a balloon.

"When I first got to the hospital I couldn't
talk about this without crying. Now it's like
I'm just talking to you about cookies or something, I don't feel it.

"Nothing like this every happened in
Brownsburg before. They couldn't believe it.

They didn't want to talk about it. They're glad to be rid of me."

i v

"I shot my father on a Tuesday. The Gideons came to the Randolph County Jail on Thursday. They asked me Are you a Christian? And I said no, I'm a Methodist. I didn't know what they meant.

"They said there's a way, a light, something to strive for.

"So now I'm in prison and it's OK, I'm happy to be here. The Lord has taught me that there doesn't have to be crime if everyone would remember the Golden Rule. The Gideons came and saved me."

The men's prison is cold and metallic. I don't know who it was that called architecture frozen music. Maybe Frank Lloyd Wright. The music of the men's prison is dissonant and cacophonous. Angry and sharp, a music you don't want to listen to for very long. The men's prison is one of the most dangerous places in the world.

I talked to an eighteen-year-old boy, a fragile, thoughtful, frightened boy. His mother was visiting. She was in her late thirties with long brown hair and braces on her teeth. Her son will be in prison, ineligible for parole, until he's in his fifties, older than she is now; this will be almost all the life he'll ever know. The first few years of that time he'll spend in protective custody, locked away from other inmates in a kind of solitary. He wouldn't last for one day outside of it. What do we demand from him, and why? We demand time, his only life, and the time we ask for at age eighteen is linear and seems to stretch on forever.

What were you like before? I asked, that you needed to be saved. He was an honor-roll student, in *Who's Who in American High Schools*. "I did well on my tests," he said, "but I didn't do any homework. My favorite subjects were math and science. Now it's psychology. I was going the way of the scientist before I came here; I was on the path to atheism. It didn't make sense to me that you get an education and work and then you die at seventy. I didn't see any point to doing anything."

"You were depressed," I said to him. "That's the way you see things when you're depressed."

"When you first get to jail, you try to keep yourself happy. You don't think about anything emotional. When, after a while, you accept it as your home, then you start looking at what you did."

"He has a stack of letters from one of the

Gideons," his mother said. We were sitting at a table in the visitor's area. There was a Polaroid picture of her son drying in the center of the table. "She told me that the first time she went to see Jeff she imagined this long-haired crazy guy, a father killer. She asked 'Does anybody wanna pray?' and this clean-cut boy came over.

"He was a victim in his home and in the trial, and now here.

"I tell him that now he's here, he should find his gifts."

"I'm a big J. R. R. Tolkien fan," he said. "I kind of somehow believe that there are elves somewhere.

"I write stories. I play *Dungeons and Dragons* with my best friend. He's in the cell below mine. We pass notes between us on string.

"My Dad was really against the game."

"You played it before you came here?"

"They accused me at the trial of being a devil worshiper. They accused my mother of running a satanic cult."

"It was like the Hatfields and the Mc-Coys," she said. "The whole town was split."

"My Dad was the salutatorian of his high school class, he was a businessman, a controller."

"He was abusive," the mother says. "I had to leave him.

"But I never said anything bad about him to the children."

"What else do you talk to your friend about?" I asked him.

"We read the Bible a lot, and Revelations. And we talk about things like whether it's worthwhile to be good, what that means and how we do it. We talk about that a lot, because there are all these temptations here."

"Like what?"

"Guys put ads in the personals and get women to write to them and send them money, things like that."

"You know," his mother said, "sometimes at night I'll dream about Jeff being here, and I want to rescue him so bad it jerks me wide awake, and I wake up crying.

"You know," she said, "I never question whether there is a God. But sometimes I question whether he cares for me or not."

v

Six women stand in a suburban kitchen. There's apricot punch and rum-spiked wassail and mounded plates of candy. My friend Alice shows us a row of wreaths stacked against the wall in the family room; she's made them for her cousins, collecting and drying the herbs and flowers, twisting them with ribbon onto metal wire. Alice's three children are teenagers. I wish I had the time to do things like that, Julie says to her. I can't wait until my kids are older.

It's the day after the party at the women's prison. I'll talk about it some but mostly I'll hold back and wonder why. Partly I suppose it's for the same reason men my father's age didn't tell war stories to their wives, the same reason parents hide painful truths from their children. It never seems like the right place or the right time, and the stories seem so out of kilter with the life in front of you. You tell yourself, finally, that you're protecting them. But you know that's not completely true, and that innocence is only touching in children.

And partly it's this: that whenever I've felt righteous indignation about anything I've found out later that it was always much more complicated than I thought, that there was something, some fact or motivation, that I hadn't known. I'm always waiting for the knowledge of my ignorance. And particularly here, in the case of crime and punishment. A woman shot her child. A woman shot her husband. A boy shot his father. What do their reasons have to do with it? Who knows what's true? Maybe their reasons appeared after months and months of going over the story in

their heads, so that it changed little by little until it was something they could live with. If I
had been the judge, what would I have done
with them?

I don't know. I only know that the number
of prisoners has doubled in Indiana in the last
ten years, that it's tripled in California, that
there are prisons within driving distance of
where I'm sitting writing this that are on Am-
nesty International's list of human rights viola-
tors, that there are more imprisoned blacks per
capita in the United States than there are in
South Africa. I can give you reasons why. I can
quote statistics, gather arguments from advo-
cates of both prisoners' and victims' rights.

But in the end this essay isn't really about
prisons. It's about prisoners. And imagination:
how difficult it is sometimes, in the midst of
the circle of your own life, to see or to let yourself see another human being as real. How
sometimes all a person needs is the ability to
vision a world outside the one he feels so
trapped in that he'd kill to get outside of it.

This is such a wonderful house, Julie says,
and that's where we focus: on the wooded
yard, the two fireplaces. It's on a hill on the
west side of town, above Crooked Creek. A
large picture window looks out into the trees.
Alice and her husband have spent hours painting and wallpapering, refinishing the floors

and moldings. The wood floors shine until
they burn, incandescent. There's something
about the light in the house; it's always shim-
mering between a warm gold or a blue. Like all
the darkness has been siphoned off and pooled
someplace far outside of it. A wonderful house.
Her three children are imaginative and gentle.
The husband handsome and kind. Alice herself
is generous and lively, with a face as bright as a
candle. The walls of her house are sound; they
seem to hold the chaos out. It's hard to imagine anything but happiness in this house.

But this is what will happen:

Two months after Christmas, my friend
Alice's youngest son will break out all the windows in the house and hit his older sister's
beautiful face hard enough to break a bone.
And what was imaginative will seem, in retro-
spect, odd, and what was gentle will seem
withdrawn. And there will be months in a hospital, and hours spent in restraints, and the
years of shuffling between one drug and another, one diagnosis and another. Age, illness,
class, his parents love, all are things which will
keep him out of jail. But the doctors will rec-
ommend a different kind of confinement.
Spirit this child away, they'll tell his parents,
and blot the space he occupied with light. And
none of her friends will understand it or even
want to talk about it. Because we've all built
similar houses, and what keeps them sturdy is

our faith in them. When life happens to us like this, isolation is the price we pay for the illusion of safety. We can't begin to talk about something we refuse to see.

But we don't know any of that on this night. There's only Christmas, the cinnamony smell of cider.

We move into the dining room and begin the cookie ritual. We each open our own container of cookies, and we hand out our recipes. We hold the empty red boxes that Alice gives us, and we circle around the table, taking a dozen cookies from each plate. Peppernuts, sweet lemon stars, springerle, and wedding cakes. Something presses at the windows, at the cracks around the doors. Now and then there will be a temporary traffic jam when two of us stop to talk and then forget to move. Keep moving ladies, one of us will say, and we'll keep on turning in the circles of our innocence.

in the suburbs

The axis of reality runs slowly
through the egotistical places—
they are strung upon it like so
many beads.

—William James

My mother is mentally ill, and I'm a writer.

When I wrote that sentence, I had to fight the urge to say *because*. Around either clause—Because my mother's mentally ill, I am a writer, or even, my mother's mentally ill because I am a writer—a sort of primal guilt I fall into all too easily. Substitute any other name and any other disaster and any other tense but leave "because I'm a writer," and it's guaranteed that I've felt that guilt at one time or another—My children will be miserable because I am a writer, my marriage will fail because I am a writer, my grandmother will die of loneliness because I am a writer, my students will remain uneducated because I am a writer. The list is endless. (Actually, substitute "my mother's mentally ill" for "because I am a writer" and the sentences feel equally true.)

Somewhere along the way I made too much of a connection between illness and creativity in all sorts of ways. Writing stories, I've thought at various times, saves you from madness, or pushes you too close to it. Writing stories has seemed like a way to understand pain as well as a way, at times, to run from it.

There are some obvious differences between the language of madness and the language of art—one is a closed system with a shaky bridge between the self who creates and the rest of the world, and the other is a form of communication, no matter how quirky or how difficult. In one, words sometimes seem to lose complete touch with meaning and attempts to regain the connection are heroic, but futile—like Peter Pan losing his shadow and trying to affix it with soap—and in the other, the words, no matter how ambiguous, mean something to someone else. "Communication," as Flannery O'Connor said, "suggests talking inside a community."

At its worst, the language of the mad is as close, I suppose, as we can come to nonsense, and it forms a community of one. Language loses all pretense of reference and becomes purified, in a way, distilled sound. Psychiatrists call this "glossolalia." Fundamentalists call it "speaking in tongues." Mothers, when their infants do it, call it "learning to speak." There are examples of this in literature—Anton Artaud's last book (o dedi / a dada orzoura / o dou zoura / a dad skizi) and some of Roethke's later poems. When there are recognizable words but no one else can make sense of them, they call it "word salad." No one ever thinks to call it music.

But there are so many gray areas. There are, and always have been, people who will argue very convincingly that the speech of the insane makes its own sense if we would only listen, that it communicates, but not necessarily within the world of reason and logic, not within the sense we like to have of an ordered universe. We shut ourselves outside of the community of the insane speaker, it's argued, rather than the other way around. Writers, particularly since the romantics were taken at their word—OK, if you're a mad genius, then you can go where the mad go, and we'll treat your art as a symptom—are sometimes accused of creating works of art which are so private they seem to have no meaning to any but the author and one or two critics, or works of art which are, perhaps, compulsively metaphoric in imagery with no apparent system behind them, but with a kind of symmetrical beauty, so what do we do with them? (I'm thinking of one or two of Eudora Welty's short stories.) But even then, it's always seemed to me that there's an authority in the voice of the creator that makes the listener believe that if only he were wise enough, or knew enough, some truth would appear to him; it's the same faith we have in the voice of the created world, that there's some method in the madness, some truth or light inside or behind it all. We lack that faith in the voice of the mad, sometimes to our detriment as well as theirs.

There are similarities which are hard to dismiss. Madness and art are both private, both involve creating narratives and symbolic systems made by bits and pieces of the culture they're born in fused to the perceptions and emotions of one individual. (Delusional systems are perhaps more culture-bound than stories; a crazy woman in China will never say she's the bride of Christ.) And they're both, in their own way, unusual callings.

For large portions of my childhood— when my mother was going crazy, or when she was hospitalized—I became a walking wound. Sick, we called it when she went away, Patricia's sick. And when she was sick I was sick as well from the loss of her. The whole time she was gone I was homesick for her; anything and everything could make me cry. That's one of the ways I got my soul so tangled up with hers it's difficult for me to disentangle it now. Because her flight into chaos was precipitated by a change in mood, any feeling—passion, anger, religious fervor—was suspect, associated in my mind with craziness and drowning. I avoid conflict at almost any cost. Look at you, people say to me, how calm you are, as my two-year-old sits on the floor playing in the suds from an overflowing washer; nothing seems to bother you. *Seems* is the operant word. Seeming is enough. In fact, I sometimes say, loss of control terrifies me, my own energy terrifies me, even happiness unnerves me, and I find myself pulling away from them. My friends smile at me condescendingly, thinking my confession is really a form of modesty, still believing I live my life in a rational calm. The number of people I've really *shown* my terror to I could count on one hand. Show it, and you're crazy. And when you're crazy, people will withdraw their love.

So. My mother had her first psychotic break when she was twenty-one. Over the years she's been diagnosed as manic-depressive, schizophrenic, schizo-affective, in all their varying terminologies. It doesn't matter what it's called. What is clear is that she gets about as crazy as you can—hears voices, decides

she's God, hallucinates, buys multiple condo-
miniums on a social security check.

When I was very young, I'd get drawn
into the craziness. We'd have some good times,
driving around to restaurants for multiple
lunches or to cemeteries to check up on old
friends. She claims now that she has never in
her life been depressed, only "high," and it was
the highs that landed her in the hospital. While
the highs were the gaudy part of her illness,
and the part that eventually resulted in hospitalization, the depression was more pervasive;
it seemed to me that it was always there. When
I came home from school, her eyes would be
red and puffy from the crying, her face lined
with sleep. During those times I felt that I
should do something to make her happy, to en-
tertain her, but it never worked. The mania, I
thought, was a result of the depression, and the
depression (I thought) was because of the
neighborhood.

She was a 1950s housewife, isolated in her
suburban home from the rest of the world. All
of the mothers worked in their houses, and the
yards were too big, the houses built just far
enough apart that it was difficult to see the
other women easily, in the course of a day. My
mother had time on her hands. The women of
her generation were, it seems to me, more
caged by the houses than the women in the

generation preceding it. (I lived for a while on an old street in New Castle, where my closest friends were small-town women of my grandmother's generation. These were not wealthy women. I felt surrounded by recipes for elaborate zucchini breads and concord grape jelly from the grapes in the arbors in the back yards. These women had herb gardens, had time for their cellos and violins and all those small-town clubs. They were known for their roses and their lemon balm. They had symphonies then, and operas, and they made their own clothes. One woman made copies of oriental paintings. She made her own paint by dabbing the single wet bristle she used to draw with on the tip of a colored pencil. She spent months on each one, drew fine details in the costumes, every hair in a woman's head. The colors weren't fast, and most of her drawings have faded. It didn't matter to her.) There's a difference between entrapment and enclosure. Neither one is good, God knows, but one is a little better than the other. A lot of what the women could do had been taken away by technology, by the ideal of the grassy suburban lawn—just try putting up a grape arbor in the suburbs, or bringing in some sheep, or Rototilling for tomatoes without hiding the garden at the back of the yard behind some bushes. And they had to spend a lot of time driving the children from place to place.

At any rate, we never talked about her illness to our neighbors or our friends, all of us working like crazy to keep the facade of middle-class suburban order and sanity, like a shaky Hollywood set, from falling down on top of us. We were all mad wizards, terrified the screen would fall away and people would see us where we were standing, in neither Oz nor Kansas, outside the net of safety, at the edge of the universe, the place where everything dissolves. So we wildly pulled our levers and our gears because a seeming world, a false world, was better than no world at all. We split the world in two that way; there was the world of forms, and then there was the truth behind that world. The inner chaos didn't matter (and, by extension, what you felt or believed didn't matter) as long as the surface was intact. Our yards were perfectly weedless. Our churches were pale blue, light wood, clear windows that only let the light in. There's a line in a poem by Tomas Transtromer: "You live well / The slum must be inside you." Nowhere is that more true than in an American suburb in the 1950s.

There was, and is, in the cleanliness of the suburbs—the old people off in nursing homes, the crazy in psych wards, the sick and dying in hospitals, the children in school—a fanatical belief in niceness, in reason and perfection. This is the New World. Good came into the world here clean and slick. Original sin never made the trip across the ocean, and certainly didn't cross the continent with the covered wagon and the dishes; somewhere along the way we shook it loose. Jung said that "nothing that is good can come into the world without directly producing a corresponding evil." To a young person building a family in an American suburb in the fifties, that statement would seem like nonsense. Evil was Nazi Germany. Goodness was the ranch house that enclosed your family in safety and isolation. But if good has been torn away from evil, how do we explain suffering? It doesn't compute. It's not possible. So hide it, and maybe it will move on by.

In many ways, an American suburb is the logical result of what Foucault called "the Great Confinement," the increasing tendency, from the seventeenth century on, to distance ourselves from what Roy Porter in *A Social History of Madness* calls "the weird and worrisome people . . . the perverse and peculiar. . . ." Foucault notes that "All over Europe the eighteenth and nineteenth centuries witnessed a proliferation of schools, prisons, houses of industry, houses of correction, workhouses and, not least, madhouses to deal with the menace of unreason." The fact that my mother has lived as long as she has in the suburbs is maybe remarkable. With her own mother as coach, she somehow perfected her suburban mask; it was good enough to pass. She was an escapee, a pod person from *The Invasion of the Body Snatchers,* loose among people who were real.

When my mother's manic episode turned scary, as it always did, I thought it was because the story she was telling herself grew more scary. The world is going to end now, she'd believe, so let's hide under the grand piano. O'Connor said that belief is the engine that makes perceptions operate. I think now that the fear came before the story, but back then I thought the story brought the fear. I saw a green shaft of light, she'd say, and it means I'm to be a prophet.

Sometimes I became a piece of the story. "God is punishing you," my mother would tell me, "because I spent the night once in a motel with a man whose breath smelled like milk."

When she was young, she had plans to be a concert pianist. She had been a music major in college, and I remember her attacking the piano keys with this incredible passion. She had small hands, like Liszt, but she could stretch them as wide as a man's. Small hands, but she could play Rachmaninoff with this crashing whirling sort of roar that touched a place in me that felt that roar like some sort of underground rushing glacial river. When she played, there was no dullness. Everyone else seemed half alive to me, but she was a burning flame.

Most of my earliest memories are of my mother playing the piano, and of me sitting down by the brassy pedals, using my hands to change the sound. I could mute it, or make each note separate, or I could press the hold pedal until all the sounds merged so that it was, down underneath the blond wood, as though all the children in the world had been let, one by one, into an echoey room to scream. At that age, in many ways, I didn't want her to play. You gave birth to me, I thought, with childish narcissism, and here I am, better than those keys — play *me*.

I saw her then as one of those Irish-looking dark-haired beauties from the movies or Disney cartoons, like Rose Red, and I felt like a pale turnip when I saw myself beside her in a mirror. But she had no silver screen in which to play out her passions, only a constricted keyboard of seven or eight notes that she was allowed to play. She married a conservative midwestern man (musical himself, but a mournful trombone musical). His sister, my aunt, was like my mother's (evil or good, depending on who you talked to) twin — beautiful, black-haired, a writer, an alto like my mother. For a while they sang in the same church choir. But she wore feather boas and black silk dresses. She left one Presbyterian minister to marry another, ended up living in the Florida Keys with her new husband, in an incredible house, and no visible means of support beyond writing the occasional drugstore detective novel. For a while she and her husband had a radio show, and once, when I was young, there was a picture of them standing beside their airplane on the front of a supermarket magazine. I remember that they wrote a book together with the subtitle "A Presbyterian Minister and His Wife Talk about Sex." My father kept his copy locked in a basement cabinet, with his whiskey. One time, when they visited us, my aunt was up on a ladder that my mother was steadying, and later, my mother told us that she hadn't been wearing underwear. God knows what she was doing up on a ladder in a dress, but I think that, finally, my mother envied her. I think that my vision of a creative adult woman caromed between those two poles—the bad girl who lived completely and happily outside the conservative Midwest, and the good one who lived miserably, did as she was told, and now and then went bonkers.

As the years went by, my mother played the piano and sang only when she was going mad, so that the music became a sign of her illness to all of us, like the way she obsessively tapped her cigarette against an ashtray. When she was well, she dusted the keys. So in a grand leap of childish illogic, that the music caused the illness, I associated what was best in her with what was the most destructive. I've done that with a lot of things. Because the content of her delusions was religious, I've been both attracted to and terrified by religion, sure that religious feeling is suspect and, like the music, another blind alley where madness hides, waiting to drag you in.

If I'm honest, now, my mother's delusions have usually made complete sense; they were just based on premises that would get her into trouble. Her life has been an immense struggle, but it has, in some ways, been a spiritual one. Always, no matter how odd it may seem, God has been her ultimate concern. Another one of the confusing ironies for her children was the rapidity with which she was locked away when God-talk came from her mouth, and how "well" she was supposed to be when complacent, when her main topic of conversation was wallpaper or a 30 percent-off sale on gold jewelry at the mall. (And this is true—she was the only adult I knew during the Vietnam War who was against it.)

"A certain tendency to insanity has always attended the opening of the religious sense in men, as if they had been 'blasted with excess light,'" Emerson said in his essay "The Over-Soul." Religious leaders, according to William James, "have known no measure, been liable to obsessions and fixed ideas; and frequently they have fallen into trances, heard voices, seen visions, and presented all sorts of peculiarities which are ordinarily classed as pathological."

George Fox, founder of the Quakers, heard voices, saw blood flowing in alleys, was about as clinically "pathological" as they come, but he founded a religion characterized by silence, community, and civil responsibility. Mother Ann Lee, founder of the Shakers, heard voices and developed compulsive rituals and laws. (Always pray with the left thumb over the right. Never the right thumb over the left. Always kneel with the left knee first. Bedsteads should be painted green. Blue and white thread should generally be used for marking. It is unnecessary to put more than two figures for a date.) Religious meetings were full of wild Dionysian dancing and song, but she left a legacy of simplicity, of lives where beauty and function, leisure and work, were far more integrated than in most communities. The list of "crazy," by our standards, religious leaders is as long as history.

James joins with other writers in seeing the things that poets, lovers, madmen, and fanatics have in common: an extraordinary emotional susceptibility and intensity, "These experiences we can only find in individuals for whom religion exists not as a dull habit, but as an acute fever rather"; a tendency to fixed ideas and obsessions; the ability to be possessed by ideas, to want to "inflict them on

their companions"; the drive to translate con-
ceptions into belief and action; and a love of
metaphysics and mysticism, which "carries
one's interests beyond the surface of the sensi-
ble world." "If there were such a thing as in-
spiration from a higher realm," James says, "it
might well be that the neurotic temperament
would furnish the chief condition of the requi-
site receptivity."

At some level, even as a child, I suspected
that. We would study history in school—the
children's crusades, Joan of Arc, Lincoln,
Churchill—and it would confuse me. Lincoln
in a profound depression. Tolstoy depressed
and then wildly religious. Why did such-and-so
in history walk around with people listening to
him, when my mother, who stands up in
church and says she's had a vision, is driven
straight to the hospital? (James's sense of the
difference rested in the vision's "luminousness,
reasonableness and moral helpfulness" as well
as on the ability of the revelations to become
part of the environment, for the rest of life to
connect with or confirm them.)

At times I thought that religion made you
mad, and at other times I thought that if ideas
came from people who behaved the way that
mad people behaved, that there must be something wrong with the ideas. Again, there were
huge flaws in my logic, but flaws I think that
my whole culture buys in to, part of a delu-

sional system that we all accept. No one, James argues, dismisses a scientific theory because the person who thought of it was mad, even though (again, if it's true that belief drives our perceptions) for all their supposed objectivity, those theories are often seen, years later, as so integrally tied to the culture of the time.

The biggest flaw in my logic, though, was deciding that my mother was in fact her own sickness, that her madness was pathology only, probably organically caused, a "chemical imbalance." There was no human being outside of the madness, and so anything she did had to be mad. I allowed her no human qualities and so allowed none to myself. I became the worst medical materialist, believing in the body only. Stimulate a certain place in the brain with electricity, and you'll taste a banana. Stimulate another place and you'll think of seventh grade church camp, even if you never went. Of course, I thought, when I heard that in Psych 101. Of course. If someone thinks she sees God, quick, get her some Prozac.

So madness is an illness characterized by a lack of reason and by disorder. Descartes elevated mind, reason, and order; what makes us fully human is our ability to reason. It's a short step from that premise to thinking that a person who is mad is less than fully human and so needs to be excluded from the community. We don't hold the crazy person responsible for her actions, but we also do not find any meaning in her beliefs. Madness is another proof of our belief that it's a heartless, mechanistic universe, and that we are, at base, nothing but machines. So many of my friends are on antidepressants—we might as well put it in the water, like fluoride. Happiness is at least as important as our teeth. What does that do to our conception of ourselves?

Look through the Psych Abstracts for any discussion of the psyche, and you look in vain. What you find are drugs and hormones and neurons. (An example: Marian Diamond, a California neuroanatomist, noticed "a greater number of neuron-nourishing glial cells in the brains of rats with an enriched environment than in the brains of deprived rats." An examination of Einstein's brain, cell by cell, showed "more glial cells than eleven other small brains." There's a musician who wants her to have his brain when he dies, to see, I suppose, whether he had enough glial cells to classify him as a genius.) You get data, a democracy of data. Never a mention of the soul.

If the soul is the thing that allows you to say "this is Mary" when you see someone you knew once but haven't seen for years, no matter how she's changed, then I don't know what happens to my mother's soul. There is no connection between the despairing mother and the wild one, the continuous part of her hidden

someplace deep behind her eyes. If telling stories is the way you construct a consistent self—
I'm the person who loved music at four, at
fourteen, at forty, or the person who loved it
and then changed my mind because . . . then
she deconstructs herself regularly, her soul a
knitted sweater with one dropped stitch that
makes the whole piece unravel in her hands.
Sometimes I have no idea what her true self is,
or where her soul goes when it's in hiding.

And yet I do recognize her—in her kind-
ness, in the consistent threads in her delusions,
and it's maybe the illness that ties her together,
as much a part of her as her hair, something
that has to be accepted in order to accept her.

I'd like to think, as painful as it's been for
her, that the drama of her feelings has given her
something as well. When James talks about
passion, fear, jealousy, ambition, worship, and
when he talks about mystical states, he talks
about them as gifts. "If they are there, life
changes. And whether they shall be there or
not depends almost always upon non-logical,
often on organic conditions. And as the excited
interest which these passions put into the
world is our gift to the world, just so are the
passions themselves gifts—gifts to us, from
sources sometimes low and sometimes high;
but almost always non-logical and beyond our
control. Gifts, either of the flesh or of the
spirit; and the spirit blow where it listeth; and

the world's materials lend their surface pas-
sively to all the gifts alike, as the stage-setting
receives indifferently whatever alternating colored lights may be shed upon it from the opti-
cal apparatus in the gallery."

Even depression can be a gift, a necessary
gift. The problem is that there's no good place,
no good time, to unwrap it. Your children and
your employer are not going to understand
when you tell them you need a couple of years
to go down into the ashes. They will have
changed by then, and they need you now. That
sense that life is dry and meaningless, the sense
of insecurity and terror that you see in the
Book of Job, in the journals of the mad and
sane, and in stories throughout history ("You
will be left alone, unable to understand / In a
world where nothing lives anymore / As you
thought it did . . . a man sees death in things.
That is what it is to be a man. . . . For being
human holds a special grief of privacy within
the universe."—*The Epic of Gilgamesh*) has
been a thread woven into any examined life.
After you've experienced a profound depression, nothing ever looks the same to you again.
Any happiness that comes afterward is not—
again, this is James, reflecting on Tolstoy's
depression—"the simple ignorance of ill, but
something vastly more complex, including natural evil as one of its elements." In the end, it

should be redemptive. You die in the old life and are reborn in the new one.

I don't know.

So I wonder about the soul, whether there is in fact a function and a place for madness.

The fact that matter is, at the subatomic level, no more than a dream of light is not the least bit troubling to me. I grew up watching my mother periodically dissolve into her own particles, like a bubble bursting into glitter.

Sometimes we're exhausted by the unpredictability of the disease, with the work it takes to undo its effects. Over the years I've returned cars for her and sacks of clothing and knick-knacks. (One year, at Easter, she bought out practically an entire crafts store, her car so stuffed with sacks of bunny parts and plastic eggs and pipe cleaners and He Is Risen magnets that she could barely drive home.) That same year she followed the hologram on her credit card down through Georgia, buying rooms full of furniture and dulcimers, ending up, finally, in Florida, where she got lost in a rainstorm looking for fresh tomatoes, the down payment checks for two time-share condos and a Mustang convertible poised and ready to bounce. There were photos of her smiling giddily in groups of complete strangers as though they were long-lost relatives, along

with a sort of Rolodex last will and testament
on index cards (an eternal flame by her father's
grave, a rose every day on the grave of the
founder of her college sorority) in her purse.
My brother had to fly down to Florida to find
her.

We've taken her to the hospital after an
overdose, taken her for outpatient shock treat-
ments, I've kept her checkbook (badly),
dressed her when she was so catatonic you
could mold her into any position like a clay
doll. And I've seen her incandescently beautiful, chain-smoking in a fury of brilliant, ecstatic talk.

When I was in my early twenties and I
grew near the age of my mother's first psychosis (postpartum, the day of my birth), I
watched myself as if I were my own physician.
I passed the date safely. No psychosis. I had
two children, so fearful of that chasm on the
other side of labor that I wouldn't dilate. Two
c-sections. No psychosis. And I'm still watching, always watching, thinking at some level
that the writing is a kind of craziness, that I'm
pulling a scam on a world that seems to at
times welcome my craziness, and I'm aware,
always, of the connections between the two.

*My mother is in the hospital, and we're
riding up together in an elevator. She's dressed
in bright red sweats; her right hand has a*

*tremor from the drugs. I close my eyes and feel
the braille dots by the floor numbers, to see if I
can tell where one number stops and the next
begins. You're pretending that you're blind, my
mother says to me, and I say yes. She's working on a delusional system, and I'm working
on a story, and I wonder what the difference is
between them.*

There is clearly a genetic basis for affective
disorders, and the same gene also seems to produce artists. The list of writers and other artists
who had a mood disorder, or who had close
relatives who did, speaks for itself. Roethke,
Lowell, Plath, Nijinsky, Steinbeck. Robert Bly
tells a story about the poet James Wright coming to his house so manic that Carol stole his
false teeth and put them in ice so they could
take a break from his talking. Graham Greene
gave credit to his bipolar illness for the emotional range of his novels. Roethke, in his
manic phases, would lecture from the class-
room window. Marguerite Young claims she
ran into him once in a hotel in Indianapolis,
and he told her to meet him in the lobby at
4:00 so he could marry her. It was the first
time they'd met.

Psychologist Nancy Andreasen did a study
involving University of Iowa writing students
several years ago and found that the percentage of those with mood disorders was signifi-
cantly higher than the general population. Of

fifteen writing students she studied, ten had what she would consider mood disorders. All reported mood swings. The percentage of writers, she estimates, who are treated for mood disorders reaches as high as 80 percent.

Kay Jamison, another psychologist and an expert in bipolar illness, surveyed forty-seven of the top British writers and artists and found that 38 percent had sought treatment for mood disorders. (Poets topped the list. One-half of the poets reported either drugs or hospitalization. Playwrights were the most likely to seek the talking cure; two-thirds of them had gone in for counseling.) Many scientists speculate that there is a genetic marker for manic-depressive illness. Why would the same gene that produces dissolution also produce form?

I'm going to invent a character now. Let's say her name is Alice, and lately she's felt like Job. Her husband left her years ago, and when she had to go into the hospital for surgery, let's say, her young son moved into a trailer with alcoholic motorcycle riders because he was too young to stay by himself. When she's released, she finds that her son is so attached to the motorcycle riders that he won't come home. She goes back to work but loses her job because the school calls so much about her son's truancy, and she goes home to find she's been evicted from her apartment, and then gets a call saying her best friend has died.

She has a boyfriend, and the next day he tells her he won't be seeing her again, and as he leaves, she feels this lightening, a sort of quiet joy like the flush of freedom she felt the first time she left her baby with a sitter and went out on her own. For a moment there's this sense of freedom, one of the burdens lifted. In the loss there's an initial exhilaration, her problems reduced temporarily by at least a third, she thinks, and she pictures what she will do with the space that's now open to her — plant a garden, knit a dress, go back to school.

She goes to sleep easily. But then begins a night of frantic dreaming.

Her dreams aren't pleasant, and she's always running — up a set of steps covered with cats, with something in her mouth that she thought was food, but it's turned bitter and grainy, and she can't swallow it. She runs into a rest room and goes behind a curtain — it's like a dressing cubicle outside a shower at a pool, a drain on the floor. She grabs a towel and spits out whatever's in her mouth, the taste of acids, and there in front of her is a woman she didn't know was there. She puts on her pleasant, social mask. Hello, she says, and how are you. A boy looks over the top of the curtain. And so this is your son, hello, I'm pleased to meet you.

She remembers there are pregnant women around all of those cats, that cats give you toxoplasmosis and the babies could be born monsters. She needs to run outside and warn them, and she starts to run, but something jerks her hard, like a hand on the cord of a lightbulb, awake.

She doesn't finish the dream.

At the zoo there's a pool with one glass wall, and you sit on concrete steps in a cool building and watch the glass. It's this beautiful shade of blue. Behind the glass the polar bears swim, their hair fanning out and flattening with the grace and sway of underwater plants. In that cool white room with only a blue glass wall holding the world of water separate from the sunlit oxygen-filled space where you breathe, now and then a polar bear will swim down hard to the bottom of the pool and shove against the floor with his great white feet. And all the heavy weight of him will shoot up through the water and into the green upper world in a fountain of silver beads, like balls of mercury. There's an effort in the transition from one world to the next, but once he's there, he moves as easily in the green world as he did in the blue one.

In that same way, grief rose through the woman's dreaming mind and forced her up to the conscious one, where she felt it so acutely that she shook with it, and it was both grief and rage. And it wasn't for just this loss, but for every loss, for all the losses, past and future, and she couldn't look away from it.

She thought of the grief rising up in her like a bear, and she could go back to sleep. It wasn't a real bear; it was *like* a bear, and seeing the connection was like a drug to her. She could sleep. And this is the next dream she had: She's in her friend's house, and they get a phone call. A disembodied phone, not connected to any outlet. He's coming, the voice says, the burglar's on his way. Her friend gathers the children in the center of the house, and the dreamer is the one who moves around the house and checks the windows. The bedroom windows are wide open, only a thin screen between the dark outside and the light within. The dark air is cold and clammy, and she pulls the windows shut; she locks the doors to keep the thief outside, where he belongs.

Grief, any passion, pulls images to itself as though it were magnetized. It wants to be made incarnate, to be in this world, and understood. It happens in dreams the way it happens in stories and in madness. As the grief rose up the first time through and made its trip through the unconscious, it pulled images of terror with it—of the mask that hides illness and death, of poison. The first dream ends with a warning—the babies will be monsters— and the dreaming mind needed, somehow, the conscious one to help shape the grief, and it shook her awake and asked her to remember the dream or write it down. The woman needed to recognize it as grief, to weave the conscious and the unconscious together. In the next dream, then, the children are safe within.

Passions rise up through images like the polar bear rises through water or the way you make swirled marbelized Easter eggs, colors mixed with oil floating on top of water, the white egg rising up through the colored oil and coming out coated fantastic colors like those wonderful swirled balloons. (When I picture the universe being created from a word, that's what I picture—the word, a feeling, rising up through a swirl of primal dust, bursting out in a rush of stars and planets. I read once that scientists think that the initial building blocks of matter were three elements. One was helium, one lithium, and I forget the third one. Helium to lift you up. Lithium to make you forget you were ever high enough to see the face of God.)

The egg rises through images and it also moves from the silence of the water into a world of sound—the child exclaiming at the colors, a radio in the background, the sound of someone's lawnmower, an airplane overhead, the barking of a dog, the gurgle of an aquarium. Feelings coat themselves in images, and they coat themselves in sound. Sometimes the sound is music and sometimes language.

The processes of creating a story or dream or delusion are probably the same.

One of the characteristics of mania is a grandiosity way out of proportion to anything. So let's say that's the feeling that needs to be embodied in myth, in story. To simplify it, let's say you wake up feeling grandiose (or rather, let's say you started the day grandiose since, if you're manic, you probably haven't slept; my mother claimed that she never had a dream). You're a Western woman, so one large pot of symbols your egg can rise through is biblical.

The man on the radio talks about the up-coming Kentucky Derby. You imagine the horses and the riders, and it catches your fancy. You think about running down to Lexington, drinking mint juleps, maybe even becoming a jockey, winning the race yourself. The weath-erman gives a prediction—another summer of drought. You hear that there was an earth-quake in Bolivia. Horsemen, you think, drought, earthquake, and you're grandiose so you assume that maybe this is all a message for you, a message God's been waiting all of eter-nity to give someone, waiting until you were ready to hear it, until you'd become the one and only instrument alive in the world tuned to the frequency of His voice. You go over to the Bible, read Revelation again. Right away, there's a mention of Alpha and Omega. You were in the Alpha Chi Omega sorority in college, and suddenly it all fits, and you get that same spooky rush that you often get from coincidences—drought, horsemen, college sororities—obviously, today you will witness the end of the world. So you take your child, and you hide her under the piano, or you call the radio station, or you go to the mall and sing.

You've selected images from among the millions of sensations that come at you, you've clumped them together, and you've strung the images as easily as you would string a beaded necklace. In much the same way, a story or a theory is constructed, image by image, fact by fact, into a whole that reconciles everything observable. You take a feeling—sexual repression, say, mixed with stagnation—and let it pull groups of images to itself—say, again, horses, and maybe water, and men. Drop those images along the path of a narrative about, well, how about that doctor you met the other day, and a woman who reminds you of your wife, and you end up with something like Lawrence's "Horse Dealer's Daughter."

It feels to me that there is something in the mind that is like that flap in the heart, that valve that makes sure the blood flows in the right direction, that keeps it from flowing back into itself. In the mind, the flap allows the bear to move from blue to green. Sometimes the mind's flap is loose, cloth on rings around a thin pole, and the flow of symbols moves easily from one world to another, feelings transformed easily to images. There's maybe a gene for that kind of flap; it allows for large leaps between one thing and another, and it sometimes is controlled and beautiful, and sometimes not.

In some, the flap is metal and larger than the hole it covers. It may begin that way, or it may happen out of fear of what's on the other side. Some people get stuck in abstraction, the flap so rigid it won't allow the symbols to be transformed, to attach themselves to the concrete world they will die without. That in itself is a kind of craziness.

Schizophrenics stay stuck on the other side of that flap, in a world so literal that an apple is an apple, an orange an orange, and there's no category, no abstract group called fruit to tie them together. A schizophrenic feels like a machine and IS a machine, feels as grand as Christ, and IS Christ. Sometimes whole groups of people go insane, turn the fear of their own deaths into something literal and decide, for instance, that the world will end on a certain day at a certain time, and they gather together on a mountain or in a church basement, waiting for the killer tornado or the cataclysmic earthquake, the wrath of God. After a while, the "like" comes back in. It was a simile mistaken for literal truth. The terror of my own death feels LIKE this, but isn't this, and they come to their senses slowly, one by one.

There's a certain joy in mistaking similes for literal truth, and a certain belief in the imagination. I talked to one of my friends who lives in Ohio during Iben Browning's earthquake scare. She said the scare had been "an Indiana thing."

"Hoosiers," she said, "have more imagination than Buckeyes." I talked to another friend who lives in Mississippi, I said to my Ohio friend, and the panic happened there as well. "Well that just proves it," she said. "There have been more Indiana and Mississippi writers than there have been Ohio ones." Only four weeks after the earthquake, the Gulf War began. If we'd been able to see the scare as a metaphor for something we all were feeling, we probably wouldn't have been the least bit surprised.

We know that matter is dottily chaotic, but the human brain won't let that be so. We tie things together in nets—that clump of dots a table, this clump of light myself. The human mind both fights chaos and welcomes it, and it's maybe the simile that saves us, that tempers what Coleridge called the esemplastic gift, that thing that makes you want to pull perceptions together like cells. Maybe it's the esemplastic gift gone bad that's crazy, and every time we take things in and move toward form—in art, in religion, in dreams—we're risking dissolution because we're diving *in*. But it's the only place we can go, finally, it's a risk we have to take, we have no choice.

And so there are those strange border areas between insanity and wisdom—the medieval nun who's crazy but who brings back visions. Some go crazy and come back empty, some come back with gifts. Some speak in tongues and are uninterpretable. Some make divinest sense.

Jung calls dreams and cases of insanity "eclipses of consciousness"—a wonderful image, the dark shadow of the unconscious for a moment darkening our conscious will. The unconscious is concrete and objective; it speaks in images. Consciousness loves abstractions, order, and systems. Separated, one is blind and the other empty. It's the job of the artist to bring to the surface what we ordinarily "evade or overlook or sense only with a feeling of dull discomfort." The hard work of the artist is in binding them together, traversing those two worlds without getting lost in one or the other.

Often what the artist brings back is something we don't want to see, and in this crazy century, that's been particularly true. So we've said that, instead, it's the poet who's crazy, and we study him or her to prove to ourselves that it's true. We turn vision into symptom. Jung again: "The frightening revelation of abysses that defy the human understanding is dismissed as illusion, and the poet is regarded as a victim and perpetrator of deception." So we "turn again to our picture of a well-ordered cosmos."

One of the differences between Catholicism and Protestantism is how close you get to all of this. "This IS my body" is too scary for a Protestant, too close to mystery, to wildness, so in the sixteenth century, or thereabouts, we snap the world in two as easily as you'd snap a cookie. And suddenly everything's a symbol, it's LIKE my body, and this grape juice is like wine which is like blood, but twice removed. The cross is symbol, empty, bare and smooth and easy to take. It's a split that made it easier to categorize, much easier to theorize, but some of our potential mystics are probably locked away because we will not allow ourselves to have faith in them. If Margery Kempe were alive today, or Julian of Norwich, we know where they would be.

I'm not saying that a psychosis is not frightening, or that we should listen to lunatics; there are plenty of historical examples in our century to prove a theory like that wrong, and my mother's pain and confusion are real. What I do think, though, is this: that my mother might have had a better life if, at some point, she'd been taught to live within the illness, to ride it like a rocking ship, or if our family had acknowledged it earlier, or if there were a place for it in our culture, some discipline to filter the mental illness through, like panning for precious minerals—a lot of sand and water drain through the colander, but now and then you're left some gold. Some disciplines teach their students what to do with hallucinations. In Zen, for instance, if you think you see God, you're to spit in his face. In an American suburb of the 1950s, a crazy woman wasn't taught a thing; she was shocked and drugged and locked away. ("There's no way out," Louis Simpson writes in his poem "In the Suburbs." "You were born to waste your life. / You were born to this middle class life / As others before you / Were born to walk in procession / To the temple, singing.")

One evening last winter my brother and I met for dinner in a hospital cafeteria, my mother locked away on the second floor. She'd unintentionally overdosed on psycho-neuroleptics. She was confused, she needed to be in the hospital, but she wanted to go home.

The doctor advised us to have her committed. My brother and I were meeting to decide whether or not to sign the papers that would do that.

There are things about the loss of freedom in mental hospitals which are exaggerated in movies, but which are troubling. The staff does turn over a lot, particularly in a long-term state hospital, where she might be moved, and they're not paid well. They're frustrated and angry and, at times, they do take that out on patients. Every year or so there's a scandal.

The citizens of Indiana refuse to put money into mental health, and the state hospitals are physical wrecks — holes in the walls, filthy screens on the windows, isolation rooms with a single dirty pallet on the floor, patients strapped to beds. I've seen them.

Even in the short-term private hospitals, like this one, there are things about behavior modification techniques, say, which bother me. No, Mrs. Jones, you may not have a cigarette (cue for the nurse to smile like Louise Fletcher in *One Flew over the Cuckoo's Nest*) because you had one twenty minutes earlier.

So we're ambivalent, torn.

I had just left a faculty meeting where we'd spent over two hours arguing, all of us stuck on the intellectual side of the flap, about the composition of a search committee. I won't go into details, but suffice it to say that we somehow got so confused over something so petty that we didn't notice until two days later that we'd ended up voting against our own best interests, if in fact there could be a best interest worth all the time we wasted on the problem. Later, we realized our mistake, and we'd go up to a colleague sheepishly and say "hey, did you notice what we've done?"

My brother is an internist, on the staff of this hospital, and on this night the vice-presidents and trustees are dressed in chef's hats, and they serve us dinner. Everyone is surface jolly, and we sit there smiling as a VP brings us pieces of chocolate cake.

One of the VPs tells us, as he pours our coffee, that he's just heard on the radio that we are bombing Iraq.

My brother and I thank him, ever the polite children, and we leave our pink table and our squares of sweet cake and go out into the hospital to look for a television.

We run by a black Yamaha piano in the lobby, roped off, electronic, the keys going up and down with all the syrupy hesitation of a piano bar pianist, but with no human being in sight, a miracle of technology.

There's a TV in the waiting room in outpatient oncology, my brother says, and we pick up speed, start jogging, me in my teacher's dress and he with his doctor's tie.

When we get to the waiting room, cancer patients and their families are standing around the TV, hushed. We are at war and maybe none of this—the cancer, the painful ties of love, will matter; somehow, we'll be free of them.

A secretary, all business, ignores the TV

and begins noisily working a copy machine. We huddle closer to the television. The news men and women are excited. The messages coming in are scattershot, many of them un-confirmed; all we know with any certainty is the Shield has become a Storm. But it seems as though we're bombing the Garden of Eden, and they say the lights are beautiful.

We tell ourselves we have to sign the pa-pers this time. She's dangerous to herself right now, dangerous to others. We acknowledge that part of it is our own exhaustion from car-ing for her in the middle of the pressures of our own complex lives.

My brother looks at his watch. He has pa-tients to see; I have children to get home to. We head toward the elevators, ride up to the sec-ond floor, press a buzzer. A man lets us in through the locked door. A cigarette lighter sits on the nurses' station, pointed out at the pa-tients like a gun. A young girl with beautiful red hair and bright red lips lights her cigarette and smiles at us. An O.T. walks through the dayroom with a parrot on her arm.

How are the patients taking this? I ask.

They're calm, a nurse says, like in that old black-and-white movie. You know. *The King of Hearts.*

We sign the commitment papers when she hands them to us, and then we head back to my mother's room.

National Public Radio is broadcasting from the speaker above her bed.

She's rolled herself into a ball, her face as frightened as a child's. It's the end, she says, I'm so afraid. She cries with thick hiccupey gasps, and holds on to our hands.

I know how you feel, I want to say, but I don't. The world feels off, broken from its thread, to all of us.

For weeks after the first bomb fell, she lived in a new story, constructed and literalized that night out of all our fears, a sci-fi version of all her earlier stories. There's been a nuclear war, she decides. All of Ohio's been obliterated. Every night, in order to visit her, we brave the chaotic rubbled streets, and we come into the unit, coated with fallout slick as pollen.

The war continues on TV. Your days are numbered, she says to us, you poor poor children. If she closes her eyes when we leave, she says, she still can see us glow.

Susan Neville is
Associate Professor of
English at Butler University.
Her previous publications
include numerous essays
and a book entitled *The
Invention of Flight*.